Leaving God Behind

Leaving God Behind

DAVID ARTHUR AUTEN

WIPF & STOCK · Eugene, Oregon

LEAVING GOD BEHIND

Wipf & Stock
An Imprint of Wipf and Stock Publishers
199 W. 8th Ave., Suite 3
Eugene, OR 97401

www.wipfandstock.com

PAPERBACK ISBN: 978-1-7252-8523-1
HARDCOVER ISBN: 978-1-7252-8524-8
EBOOK ISBN: 978-1-7252-8525-5

Manufactured in the U.S.A.   09/08/20

Contents

CHAPTER 1

In the Middle of a Dark Wood

> In the middle of the journey of our life, I came to
> myself, in a dark wood, where the true way was
> wholly lost.
>
> —DANTE ALIGHIERI, *THE DIVINE COMEDY*

IT IS DIFFICULT TO write these words. I am full of fury. I am riddled with despair. I am also exuberant, close to the brink of tears, often these days, because of new joy I have never known until now. The truth be told, I am a mess, a total and complete mess. Maybe you are as well. Those who have an unshakeable faith, many answers, and much of life figured out will not find much of what follows in this book intelligible. This is not a book for those people. This is a book for the broken and the lost. This is a book for those who need encouragement, not in the story of someone who has found their way to the light at the end of a tunnel, but only in someone who has found the courage to share his own lostness, without gloss and without reservation.

There is freedom in confession. But real confession is hard to hear, and it is harder yet to tell. Nakedness is taboo. Exposure means vulnerability, and really, who wants to be vulnerable? When we risk openness we lay ourselves bare to the possibility of life's brutalities.

Yet only in this way are we also opened to the possibilities of the real, the deep, the eternal. Vulnerability is the very condition for the possibility of wholeness.

For my part I want to be vulnerable here. My confession is that after years as a passionate follower of Jesus Christ I did what felt like the unthinkable, something I never imagined I would do, I let go of God and I left the church. In this way my story is part of a larger story, one of people leaving religion behind. While religion as a whole continues to grow in places like Asia, Africa, and South America, in Europe and here in North America people have been leaving religion and especially Christianity behind by the droves for decades now. In the United States, for example, from 1960 to the turn of the century, the Episcopal Church lost more than 1 million members while the Presbyterian Church lost 1.7 million and the United Methodist Church 2.4 million.[1] When I left the church, however, I did so not only as a parishioner but also as a pastor. In so doing I left behind not only a profession but also an essential and intimate part of my person. I left behind an entire way of being. Ministry, like other vocations, comes with a multitude of personas, ways of viewing yourself, and various and very specific ways of being with others. Letting go of that complex of my identity was a kind of death. There was grieving. By me and also by the many people who had come to know me primarily if not exclusively as pastor.

In addition to leaving behind that complex of my identity, I also left behind a six-figure salary, an act in itself that felt close to madness. Who in their right mind does that? One should at least find another job first. That would be the logical thing to do. The safe thing to do. Or make such a dramatic move if you are living on your own, not when you have a spouse and two young children to provide for. I won't lie, it was a difficult decision to leave the church and having a stable job and salary was a part of what made the decision difficult. Money matters. But when you begin to feel like a stranger in your own life, no longer recognizing the person you are, or thought you were, you have to wonder when enough is enough.

---

1. Wilson, *Setting Words on Fire*, 8.

As I write this I am unemployed, purposefully, after serving in church ministry for the past sixteen years of my life. My last place of ministry, the First Congregational Church of Ramona, California, where I served as pastor for eight years, was a joy in numerous ways. Our church in Ramona through an abundance of deeply dedicated, compassionate individuals was flourishing. We expanded to add a third worship service, welcoming an average of twenty new members each year for eight years in a row. We launched innovative small group offerings such as Laughter Yoga and a monthly Death Café where people in the community could openly explore their questions about life and death. We built homes for the homeless in Tijuana, began a free Farmer's Market available to those in need, established a new Endowment Fund to secure our ministries for future generations, and more. These endeavors at their heart were an expression of love according to what Jesus identified as the most important commandment, namely, loving God and loving people. I felt passionate and I was dedicated to service. I enjoyed empowering others through teaching, weaving together insights from the Bible with contemporary cosmology, psychology, history, poetry, and philosophy for Sunday sermons that were eclectic, sometimes humorous, and always aimed at helping people to better care for themselves, each other, and the world. I also loved sitting with others one-on-one, caring for a widow in grief, or listening to the laments of a young man recovering from a heroine addiction. There were always challenges in my work. But I can proudly say that during my ministry with the good people of Ramona, we loved well and we loved a lot.

This made my decision to leave not just Ramona but the church as a whole an utterly difficult one. "Why David? Why are you leaving?" That was the question I received again and again from teary-eyed parishioners during my departure. The short answer was that just as I had received a clear sense of calling into ministry at the tail end of my teenage years, likewise, now, I had a clear sense of calling that something new was on the horizon, though I was not sure what that something was, a something I nonetheless knew I could not begin to claim without first letting go my present form of ministry. The longer answer to the question of why I was leaving

3

the church was one I was not ready to share with anyone at the time, save for my wife and my spiritual director, because of how personal and strange the reason was and indeed still is to this day. I was not only called to leave the church behind. Deeper still, I have left God behind. Indeed it was a calling.

Despite the contradictory nature of a calling from God to leave God (because wouldn't I still be clinging to God by listening to God to let go of God?), after wrestling with the decision for the better part of two years, and knowing our church was in a solid place for me to pass the baton of leadership to another, I let it all go. My title. My salary. My ministry. Friends and acquaintances. Everything Christian that had become so familiar. I let it go and ventured into what felt like a void.

We tend to shun emptiness in our lives. Space for inactivity. Time for being alone. Silence in conversations. These brushes with nothingness make us feel uncomfortable. But when we have a sense of something stirring us, beyond the comforts and complacencies of the present, beckoning for us to become more fully that which we are, then, embracing the void and emptying ourselves can actually be a great gift, a supreme act of self-compassion.

When I left the church and God I did not know what would come next. I only knew I was beginning to head in the right direction, even without knowing my new destination. Since leaving I have experienced something like a deep spiritual cleanse. Having emptied myself of church involvement, most religious thoughts, and spiritual practices as well, I have found myself in a no man's land unfamiliar, uncomfortable, dark, and yet, at the same time, strangely inviting and even healing.

In my darkest moments I have been tempted to think I am alone. But this is a type of conceit. My experience is by no means singular. Though no two journeys are exactly the same, though the content and contours of our stories vary, I am reminded time and again of the others also wrestling with what it looks like to live in faith beyond the bounds of religion. There are so many of us. It seems an increasing number of people are acquainted with the experience of exile and homecoming, though whereas once the traditional narrative was that of experiencing exile in life and then homecoming by conversion and adoption into a religious community, now the experience is often inverted: we live in an age of exile from religion, experiencing homecoming instead through the aesthetic and the eccentric, the digital and the natural, the intimate and the simple. I am sharing my story here for those in exile, for anyone who has ever felt a little like Alice in Wonderland or Neo in the Matrix. I want you to know that you are not alone. And while answers are far and few between, there is consolation sometimes in simply hearing the story of another whose face is your own.

While visiting the Chautauqua Institute in New York one summer I remember listening to a talk about a growing number of clergy who shockingly realize one day they have somehow lost their faith. Many of these clergy choose to keep the revelation clandestine for some time, continuing to serve their congregations because their livelihood depends on it. Given that ministers have their training in a subject area (theology) arguably more difficult to transfer to other lines of work than some, it is easy to see how these priests and pastors might feel trapped in their own professions, struggling to live authentic lives as people without faith for people with faith. Listening to the speaker talk about this phenomenon I felt a deep swell of sorrow for my colleagues. At the same time I could not relate.

I did not lose my faith. I did not leave the ministry behind because of pastor burnout or church politics and I did not leave God behind because I became an atheist. Faith to this day continues to figure prominently in my life. What has changed, however, since leaving God and the church behind is the character of my faith, faith not as a matter of assent in doctrine or even the supernatural, but faith as an ability, the ability to trust my own inner compass, the ebb and flow of my interior life and all that dwells there. Such faith has an intuitive character. It differs slightly and sometimes greatly from person to person and takes precedence over any external authority that might try to guide or misguide us. The development of my faith, internally, downward, to a rooted, deeper place of trusting and being, eventually led me to knowing that the church, pastoring, God, all of it, it just wasn't me anymore. Once I knew that, without being sure how I knew it, just that I knew it, beyond a shadow of a doubt, in a word it was "faith," I knew I had to find the courage to move on, as painful as that would be.

One of the practices that helped me along this way of letting go and moving on was writing. Historians tell us that writing first began as a form of record keeping with numbers, and then later as language, around the year 3,000 BCE in Mesopotamia, 1,200 BCE in China, and around 600 BCE in that area between North America and South America known as Mesoamerica. What's interesting is that the phenomenon of writing happened in these three places independent of each other. Writing, that is to say, seems to be a deeply human phenomenon. A longing. An instinct that defines us transcending both time and culture. The world of thought is vast beyond comparison, and the ability to express and explore our selves in narrative and ideas through the advent of writing surely holds a special place in the human experience. Writing satisfies and even amplifies an urge we have to imaginatively engage the wildness of the world. The psyche discovers a native way of being and belonging in the event of writing. When we write, openly and freely about whatever it is that happens to be stirring inside of us, curiosity is released and something magical happens, a kind of alchemy. It is almost as if the act of inscribing something, out there, onto papyrus or paper or a computer screen, elicits truth from in here, inside us, even at times truths we did not know about ourselves or previously were not ready to look at face to face. The act of writing something *down* seems to bring something *up* from within. That something might be anger, frustration, our disappointments with life, or, a glimmer of something hopeful, a secret longing in our lives we had almost forgotten, a deep desire simply to be seen, to know as we are known, a recovered innocence revealed that wants to be embraced and incorporated into the larger narrative of who we are. Writing has that kind of power.

As far back as my childhood, writing always seemed to call to me. Whether writing screenplays for my friends to enact in short films during the doldrums of summer, or discovering the strong allure of English over Math class in middle school and high school, I found joy in composition. Then, during an especially dark season leading up to my departure from the church, writing returned to me in a new manner. For some time I had been wrestling with melancholy in ways that are difficult to describe because the lowness and loneliness I felt was something other than clinical depression. One of the best images I have come across for my bouts with lassitude is the noonday demon, otherwise known in ancient spirituality as acedia, a bleak melancholic sense of existence, even when all appears to be sunny and bright, often doubling down on one's despair because of the apparent senselessness of it amidst life's blessings. Unable to ever shake this sense, I briefly toyed with the idea of seeing a therapist before coming to the conclusion my condition was not so much psychological as it was spiritual. Not that this made things any easier. Putting aside my pride and doing some research, I eventually identified a spiritual director. Whereas a therapist might help you overcome cognitive distortions or emotional challenges from your past, and a life coach will focus on getting you where you want to be in the future, a spiritual director is a guide who helps you work towards integration, a kind of harmony with the pain, beauty, and messiness of the present. I chose my spiritual director not primarily based on education or experience, though these were important factors, too. I chose her believe it or not based mostly on her appearance. Not attractiveness, mind you, but what I later learned is called physiognomy. Physiognomy is discernment about a person's character from their countenance. While at first that may sound sketchy, actually, there is strong evidence from studies of autism, nonverbal communication, and evolutionary biology showing us that quite often the eye is indeed a window to the soul.[2] There is something about a person's presence, communicated through the face, while not all revealing that nevertheless queues the ready recipient in to something profound about the other's ethos, something that cannot be contrived or concealed.

Finding a good spiritual director was such a gift. After getting to know each other and gradually building trust, my director helped me by drawing my attention back to the touchstone of writing, and to a specific form of writing. Years ago when I was a student I had read a book called *The Spiritual Exercises*, a classic of Western

---

2. Stone and Heen, *Thanks for the Feedback*, 81–84.

spirituality written in the sixteenth century by Saint Ignatius of Loyola. Until now, however, I had only read but never actually tried for myself a writing-reflection technique derived from *The Spiritual Exercises* called the Examen.

The Examen at its core involves asking yourself two simple questions. What was it today that gave me the most life? What was it today that drained me the most of life? After reflecting on each question, you write down your responses, keeping a private log.

These are elemental questions to ruminate on rather than rush through because your responses, collectively, after not long, begin providing you with a glimpse into the inner workings of your soul. To take just a little bit of time to reflect and write in this way at the day's end, as a practice before you go to bed, I learned is like sleeping with bread.

Children who were orphaned and left to starve after the bombing raids of World War II often had trouble sleeping. Those rescued were placed in refugee camps where they received shelter, food, and care. But some of these children were so traumatized by the loss of their families that they struggled nightly with insomnia, terrified of waking up only to find themselves homeless and hungry again. The caretakers in the refugee camps tried all sorts of things to put the children at ease. Nothing seemed to help. Then, one person struck upon the oddball idea of giving each child a loaf of bread, to sleep with at night. As curious as this sounds, it actually worked. It was similar to the consolation provided by holding a stuffed animal. But for these children it was even better. The bread reminded them, "Today I ate. And tomorrow I will eat again."[3]

My practice of the Examen at the end of each day likewise became a source of nourishment and consolation in the midst of my own crisis. As I began sensing the radicality of a departure from God, and that the church was no longer a place for me, writing down my reflections each night provided both clarity and reassurance that I was orienting myself in the right direction. As I wrote I found using the word "because" indispensable. I would write down where I found life and death each day, and then after writing the

3. Linn et al., *Sleeping with Bread*, 1.

word "because" clearly state *why* something had granted me life or taken it away. The identification of why I experienced something to be life-giving or life-draining required careful examination, each night, on my experiences of abundance and depletion. The examination was like reacquiring fresh eyes on my own life. It is curious how clueless we can be sometimes to our own deepest sources of reduction and regeneration. What I wrote down some nights I found completely unsurprising. Other nights, however, I did not know at first why something had drained me or filled me with life, and that itself was a gift worth unpacking. Still, on other nights, specifying why something had given me life or taken it away was nothing less than revelation.

Much like what I am writing here, most of what I wrote during that time of nightly journaling were observations I could not have anticipated. Something I have known about myself, for example, for some time now is that I listen well to others. Yet one of the things I discovered was continually draining me of life was just that: listening to the endless problems of people, and often people who really were not looking for help but just someone to unload on. Part of me felt ashamed of this revelation. "You're a pastor for God's sake," I told myself. "It's your duty, your calling, to be there for others in this way. Get over it. Deal with it." But the more I tried to will myself to be patient, allowing others to vent, reasoning that I was at least serving as a sounding board for others and fulfilling my role as a minister, the more I felt agitated and depleted. The will is funny like that. We can will ourselves to do many things, amazing things. History bears witness to the phenomenal feats we can climb by grinning and bearing it through sheer willpower. Yet, as good people like Parker Palmer remind us, we can also do great damage to others, and ourselves, by constantly willing ourselves to do this or that, to be this or that, out of some misplaced notion that we "should" or "ought to" all the while ignoring our more organic way of being in the world.[4] Moralisms run thick even still in our nihilistic culture. The voices of "should" and "ought" often come from external sources, ones that would presume to know you better

---

4. Palmer, *Let Your Life Speak*, 9–22.

than you know yourself. But you risk much when you stop listening to yourself. And you risk too much when you stop living from the truth of who you are, and likewise who you are not.

A famous rabbi by the name of Zusha once said, "In the coming world God will not ask me, 'Why were you not Moses?' God will ask me, 'Why were you not Zusha?'" We can easily contemporize and personalize rabbi Zusha's observation. "In the coming world God will not ask you, 'Why were you not more like Martin Luther King Jr. or Gandhi or Mother Teresa?' God will ask you, 'Why were you not you?'"

You are not to be like Zusha. Or Moses. You are not even supposed to be like Jesus, despite the popularity of the well intentioned but misguided "What Would Jesus Do?" saying. You are you. You are not anyone else, and the moment you fixate on being like another, any other, no matter how noble or notorious, famous or infamous, rather than being yourself, you begin going against the grain of your own inherently and beautifully unique nature. You are magnificent. There is something absolutely and wonderfully particular about who you are. There has never been and never will be another you, and the only way to live honestly with yourself, and others, in touch with your own vitality, is to live from the center of this uniqueness, rhythmically with yourself rather than against yourself. It is risky business telling yourself to be other than who you are.

I began realizing during my practice of the Examen that I had been doing just that though, slowly but surely abusing my own nature, doing a superb job of listening to many others but at the cost of doing a poor job of listening to myself. My own nature was pushing back, informing me that I had better make some real changes or be prepared to pay the price. Through my writing I began to see that though I was a good listener I had allowed myself to lend my ear to far too many people, or maybe the wrong people, unnecessarily, perhaps in part because I thought I ought to as the pastor and perhaps also in part because I was overly concerned about the judgments of others if my level of pastoral care dropped below a certain threshold. I had become known in the church for both the quality and quantity of my pastoral care and visitations, and that felt good, or at least I thought it felt good, until I began to see more clearly that this habit of mine was slowly and secretly draining me of my own essence.

There was one exception. I noticed that whenever I had the opportunity to sit, listen, and work with someone on the edge, and to have something more like an actual back-and-forth conversation with such an individual, that I found life-giving. By "on the edge" I mean someone whose life was at a precipice, emotionally, socially, physically, or spiritually. The death of a child. The loss of a job. A divorce. A cancer diagnosis. As awful as any of these experiences are, there is a very thin and fine silver lining to them, one that does not at all justify the awfulness of the experiences, nor soften the pain of their blows, yet a silver lining nonetheless. The silver lining is the fact that most of us are typically so deeply entrenched in our self-deceptions, resistant to any real change, that it is only when we find ourselves forced to the brink that then, if at any moment, the rigor mortis of our condition begins to break apart and, at the precipice, we change.

In writing, I learned whenever I had the privilege of being with those who found themselves on the edge—a man trying to find his way to sobriety, a woman wrestling with a scathing sense of life's meaninglessness—there was something enriching in the experience for me and those I sat with. These were individuals who were hurting but also who were desperate for change. They were ready for surrender. Spending time with them drew forth something good, out of both of us, like a new third element previously hidden but now unveiled through the nexus of nothing more than a meaningful conversation.

In Japanese there is a term for this kind of reciprocity—*jita-kyoei*—literally "mutual benefit." Such mutual benefit means connecting the joy of who I am with an intrinsic need or desire in who you are, in a way that enlivens both parties. In this way, rather than going against the grain of who you are, you learn to work wisely, and playfully, with those aspects of your nature that are fitting to *some* peoples' needs and desires, recognizing you cannot be everything to everyone for the simple reason that you are not everything or everyone. You are you.

During my nightly Examen, in addition to the life-giving source of being with those on the edge, I began to notice another life source, one that was less novel yet no less crucial. It is a lifeline I have sometimes felt ashamed of, or at least bashful to acknowledge. I enjoy being alone.

In our highly extroverted culture it is not uncommon to look upon someone who actually enjoys solitude as the odd one out. Society increasingly leans in the direction of the social, social media, and social networking such that someone like me can feel a little funny whenever I need a few days alone to hunker down in the hermitage of my home, or a night away from my family, or saying no to attending yet another church function that lifts up the prize of community. Our longing as human beings to find *some* people and *some* places where we discover the joy of belonging, and where we can be more or less fully our unadulterated selves, is a good pull I feel in my life as much as anybody. Still, I have gradually learned that I am at my best when I have ample time for aloneness, for simply being. It is easy, too easy, to continually ride the frenetic pace of modern life on the surface with little to no awareness of the deeper happenings within the sanctuary of your own interiority. Yet without some stillness, silence, and solitude, the soul finds it incredibly difficult to emerge, let alone engage life authentically. If you allow yourself to be bombarded by the commotions of daily life without any respite, you should not be surprised if you gradually become disconnected from your true desires, and your true self. Taking time to slow down and stop, every now and then, to actually stop, completely, to disconnect from others and our devices and the wider world, even once a week in order to rest, reacquainting yourself with your own soulfulness and your own voice, this is an invitation to the emergence of true selfhood.

What was it today that gave me the most life? What was it today that drained me the most of life? Spending time writing down my thoughts in response to these two questions each night was like tilling the soil of my soul. I was reminded how solitude is an essential energy source sustaining me, and one that I needed to honor more than I was doing. But that's a bit of a curious revelation for a pastor, a very people-oriented line of work where creating community and inviting others into a place of belonging is naturally a big part of the lay of the land. The more I wrote, and the longer I sat with the revelation of my reflections, the more I began to sense something rather unsettling: somehow, somewhere along the way of the journey of my life, I had become something of a stranger to myself, unbeknownst to myself.

The mere thought of this was deeply disturbing at first such that I could only glance at it out of the corner of my eye, from time to time, usually dismissing it as nonsense. The timing of the revelation, too, was uncanny. "Dear Lord, please agitate me. Disturb me. Make me uncomfortable that I might more clearly see and know Thee." This is an ancient prayer I had shared with my congregation one Sunday as we were traveling through a sermon series on the Uncomfortable God we encounter in Scripture. It is admittedly a strange prayer. Why would anyone pray to be agitated? Perhaps, it is because being comfortable is not always what the soul needs. The medieval poet Dante Alighieri understood this all too well.

"In the middle of the journey of our life," Dante writes, "I came to myself, in a dark wood, where the true way was wholly lost. It is a hard thing to speak of, how wild, harsh and impenetrable that wood was, so that thinking of it recreates the fear. It is scarcely less bitter than death: but, in order to tell of the good that I found there, I must tell of the other things I saw there."[5] These are Dante's opening words in the *Commedia*, one of the great poetic works of all time, better known to most of us as Dante's *Divine Comedy*. Even if you have never heard of the *Commedia* chances are you are nonetheless familiar with it, perhaps through Hollywood's adaptation of Dan Brown's bestselling novel *Inferno* starring Tom Hanks that appeared in theaters a few years back, or maybe simply in how you think about the afterlife. Dante was the one who made famous our Western three-tier conception of an afterlife comprised of heaven, purgatory, and various levels of hell. Dante, a thinker, writer, and person of Christian faith, became entangled in the politics of late thirteenth-century Italy.[6] It was a time when the intensity of the

---

5. Dante, *Inferno*, 2.
6. Whyte, "What to Remember When Waking," 17:00–18:20.

debates could endanger your very life should you end up on the wrong side of an argument. Through a confluence of events Dante one day found himself facing execution, almost, which instead became a sentence of exile. He was forced to flee his homeland of Florence. To our ears this may sound like a saving grace—banishment over execution—but to Dante it felt more like a form of death. In Italy, even to this very day, people have a strong sense of belonging to the locality. Place and personhood are intimately related such that Dante's exile was akin to a nightmare, or daymare if you are familiar with those. When Dante was forced to leave Florence about halfway through his life, it meant leaving behind a part of himself. It meant losing touch with the theological and aesthetic center of his life, not to mention estrangement from his friends and colleagues. It was a form of dying. In the midst of this dark, depleting, melancholic place, Dante begins his *Commedia* by writing, "In the middle of the journey of our life, I came to myself. . ."

It seems we do come to ourselves, uncomfortably, and confusedly so, most commonly in the middle of our journey through life. We do not need to dumb down this crucial part of our journey with psychological clichés like midlife crisis. Such labeling too often belittles the human experience. The height and width and depth of the soul's journey eludes our attempts to neatly classify and shelve what we find too messy or massive to deal with succinctly. We do well to remember that our words and classifications will always remain on the shore of our own experience, pointing to an infinite horizon interior to us that defies even our most clever attempts to limit it by defining it.

It is true as Dante recognized, and as many others recognize along their own journeys, that there is something about a midway point which provides us with a unique perspective. Whether we are imagining a walk down a pier, or watching a movie with a friend, or the point we happen to find ourselves positioned halfway into our own lives, from the midway point, this point of orientation, we are able to look back over enough of what has gone before to have at least a strong sense of what the journey is and is not about, those places where the path has been traversed well and those places with perilous pitfalls we might have avoided, or at least negotiated differently, even the humble realization that falling and failing is an inevitable part of the journey. Likewise, when we look ahead from this midpoint, though we do not know for sure what is to come, we understand more piercingly that there is an end to the story, that the journey is not never-ending, and with regards to our own journeys the choices we make going forward are absolutely precious and precarious because there is no such thing as a redo.

Though I thought I knew exactly where I was headed in my life—I had forged a strong sense of identity through my young adult and then adult years as a minister, teacher, author, martial artist, husband, and father—I was now beginning to sense I was actually completely and totally lost. So lost that I had not even known I was lost.

As my eyes began to open to this reality, it was like meeting a stranger in a dark wood who was in fact myself, wholly lost yet, curiously, not only worried but also a bit excited about being lost. It is a myth that we can only be delighted or distraught, sad or glad at any given moment in our lives. Such binary thinking overlooks the rich complexity in being a human being. In truth, as we look more closely at our experiences, we see that sorrow and joy can exist together. This of course is not easy to understand at first. Yet when we think about some of our deepest life experiences, such as being present at the birth of a child, or the death of a friend, we see that great sorrow and great joy are often parts of the very same moment.[7] The joy of a baby's birth is also the death of a couple's undivided affections, and the sorrow of a friend's passing is also the happy remembering of how because of that relationship our lives will never be the same. In a similar way, realizing I had lost myself struck me as simultaneously frightening and exhilarating. It reminded me of a time when my wife and I were lost in the woods while hiking once in Connecticut. We wandered about for some time before we even had any inkling that we were lost. After a while we began to quietly suspect we were lost but were reticent to admit as much. Then, when we knew we were lost and were willing to talk about it, Erin began to panic while at first I was close to ecstatic.

7. Christensen and Laird, *The Heart of Henri Nouwen*, 44–45.

"It's like we're on actual adventure!" I told Erin. She looked at me like I was crazy. I was confident, though, that even if it took some time we would find our way out of the woods, eventually, at least to a main road somewhere, if not back to where we had parked the car. "But what if we don't find our way out before dark?" Erin asked with concern after close to an hour of fruitless searching, the afternoon sun setting. She had a point, and I did feel some of her fear as well, especially as the reality of our situation sank in, there in that dark wood, just as I think Erin felt some of my maniacal pleasure, too. Maybe. Thank goodness, finally, we crossed paths with another couple hiking through the woods that day. They were able to point us in the right direction. We found our way.

As I began realizing my own lostness in life, I was delighted and not only despairing because of what I had learned as a Christian, how actually it is only when we are lost that then we can be found. If you are not willing to admit you are lost, or lost once again, there is little hope. But surrendering yourself to the crucible of confession creates new possibilities. There is something about confession, about telling your own truth, your own ignorance, your own brokenness, that leads you home.

CHAPTER 2

The Bedlam of Belief

Madness need not be regarded as an illness.
Why shouldn't it be seen as a sudden—more or less
sudden—change of character?

—Ludwig Wittgenstein, *Culture and Value*

In 1662 the death of the French mathematician Blaise Pascal led
to a peculiar discovery. A few days after Pascal passed, a servant
happened to stumble upon a crumpled up piece of parchment. Pascal had hidden the parchment inside one of his coats by sewing it
into the lining. He had been secretly carrying it around with him
for the last eight years of his life. Apparently it meant a great deal
to him. The words scribbled onto the parchment concerned a pivotal happening in his life. On the 23rd of November 1654, for two
hours, Pascal found himself in a trance.[1]

Most people have no doubt found themselves in a daze from
time to time, here and there, staring out a window, lost in a moment of reverie, enwrapped in a daydream. But being in a sustained
trance for two hours is really something. Pascal was a Christian and,
according to his recollection of the event, the trance was a thoroughly religious experience. Pascal encountered God. The Bible in

1. See Mlodinow, *The Drunkard's Walk*, 75–76; Rogers, *Pascal*, 4–5.

a few places describes God as a consuming fire and through and through this was Pascal's experience. It was a "night of fire" as he later recorded the revelation.

Pascal emerged transformed. How could he not? Revelation has consequences, any kind of revelation. Imagined. Real. Religious. Secular. Whether you have had a personal epiphany, gleaned insight through an immersive conversation with someone, had a divine experience, or at least thought you did, once you see something previously hidden, there is simply no going back. Revelation changes us.

For Pascal the consequence of his revelation was a new trajectory in life. He says God came to him and in the course of his trance saved him from a corrupt state. Following the experience Pascal was moved to empty himself. He sold most of his possessions. His carriage. His horses. His furniture. His books. He let go most everything, except for his Bible, selling many of his items and giving the proceeds to the poor. More radically still, beyond possessions, Pascal let go most of his friendships. He also relinquished his beloved study of mathematics. And, if that wasn't enough, he even took to wearing an iron belt with spikes on the inside, pushing the belt into himself if ever he felt too happy.

As modern people it might be tempting for us to pass judgment on Pascal, to write him off as an antiquated oddball of history. But let's resist that temptation. Pascal lived in a different time and a different culture, which might account for at least some of the perceived strangeness of his actions. Beyond that, if we give Pascal the benefit of the doubt and suppose for a moment that what he wrote down about his experience is possibly true, or at least acknowledge that Pascal thoroughly believed it to be true, then really, who is to judge Pascal? Who is to say what constitutes an appropriate response to experiencing God? When Moses saw a bush burning that did not burn up, which he understood as a divine encounter, he was moved to remove his sandals and change his entire way of life, once living in relative obscurity and with perhaps some self-consciousness about a speaking impediment, and then, suddenly, thrust into the limelight, leading his fellow Hebrews out of slavery in an exodus from Egypt. Likewise, when Jesus, still a child, sensed

God calling him one day to abandon his family, knowing it was something he had to do, no matter how outrageous it might appear to others, even his own mother and father, he did what he clearly felt he had to do. The purported experience of encountering the divine, it seems, is often rich with eccentricity, intensity, and intricacies—consequences—not only for the recipient of revelation but also for those in proximity. Pascal was no different on this account. He did his best vis-à-vis an overwhelming experience to heed his own conscience and flesh out the implications. He even continued to be quite productive because of it. After his trance, he went to great lengths to write down his thoughts about religion, God, and life beyond the parchment he carried around with him in his coat, thoughts that were later published under the title *Pensées*, a book that has been translated into numerous languages and is still in print to this day because of its contributions to philosophy, theology, and mathematics. The inception for the book was Pascal's unusual experience. We likely would not have this literary gift apart from his experience.

Divine experiences of course do not always yield noble results. Abraham's experience with God had him almost kill his own son. Modern day examples of horrifyingly similar feats include suicide bombings, genital mutilation, and gender subordination all in the name of some perceived divine command or revelation. Can divine experiences whether real or imagined be trusted? How can one gauge whether a divine experience is in any sense valid? If it is the consequences of how one lives in response to a perceived divine experience that determine its validity, then aren't we setting ourselves up for limiting "God," missing and dumbing down the very idea of God, one who is presumably greater than all things, including what we perceive to be favorable consequences and the morality we deem acceptable as our litmus test for those reporting such experiences? These are knotted questions. And the knot is far from theoretical. I was knotted by such questions after having a most unusual experience myself.

It was three o'clock in the morning. Despite my very best efforts to drift back to dreamland, I was wide awake. I am an occasional insomniac. Some nights, I simply cannot fall asleep while others I awake long before my alarm goes off, restless, knowing that closing my eyes to attempt sleep again will only end in the utter futility of too much tossing and turning. When darkness falls, my mind wanders. It made working the nightshift during my college days convenient. My mind's stubborn refusal to shut up and shut down is something I have learned to live with.

On this particular morning after slipping out of bed, quietly showering, and giving my wife Erin still asleep in bed a kiss, I jumped in my car and began heading to the church to begin my workday. Winding down the back roads of Ramona, California to the First Congregational Church where I was serving as pastor, I decided to swing by the local Dunkin' Donuts first for a cup of coffee. Happy to be pulling up to the drive-through for my morning sacrament, I was soon disappointed as I realized they were not yet open. Peering through the window to find someone, anyone, who might brew me a cup out of kindness anyway, I gave up after a minute and continued with my drive to the church.

My thoughts were thick that morning, not about church operations or stewardship campaigns or mission projects but the bigger picture of where my life was heading. For more than a year I had been going through a process, led by God I believed, of emptying myself. The technical term for this, known among Christiany speaking people in theological circles, is *kenosis*, a Greek word meaning "emptiness." According to the Bible, this is what the Son of God did for us, both as a gift and example, emptying himself, becoming a servant for all.[2] I had been operating my life for far too long in the opposite way, not emptying, but acquiring. Degrees. Titles. Advancements. Achievements. It's not that these acquisitions were necessarily a bad thing. In fact, many of the gains were fitting to my stage of life as a young adult who was genuinely enthusiastic about learning, growing, and helping others. After experiencing a spiritual awakening near the end of my teenage years, saving me from drugs, apathy, and the worst parts of myself, I soon enrolled in college, studying Christian thought at the University of Hartford and then religion at Yale Divinity School. Along the way I read and

2. Phil 2

collected a vast array of books on church history, leadership, and theology while also working my way up as a martial artist to a third degree black belt in jujitsu and a separate third degree black belt in karate. Before I knew it, I had served at churches in Connecticut, Massachusetts, New Mexico, and California, first as a part-time Director of Christian Education while also moonlighting as an adjunct professor of philosophy and religious studies at Sacred Heart University, and then eventually becoming ordained and doing full-time ministry, my life a whirlwind, other-focused, doing a lot of good for a lot of people, day after day, week after week, month after month, year after year. Counseling, baptisms, weddings, funerals, meetings, conferences, teaching, preaching, planning, strategizing. I married, became a father, wrote a few books, had my own dojo, and then, then something changed.

Change is mysterious, at once evanescent like a morning mist, and yet as reliable as the turning of the seasons or the rising and setting of the sun. Change is sometimes a reality we find ourselves in rather than something we choose. We can be deep in the midst of existential, elemental change without having intended it, and at first without much more than an inkling, an intuition that there is a happening. Sensing that I was changing, without knowing exactly why or how, I knew I needed to begin giving expression to the change. It longed for form. The change beckoned increasingly for incarnation.

Over the course of about two years, I began to flesh out this change. After much thought, I retired my role as a sensei, ending more than twenty years as a martial artist and closing the doors to my dojo in the San Diego Country Estates. It was difficult disappointing the many students I had developed relationships with who had come to enjoy training with me over the years. Yet, at the same time, I felt great peace with my decision. I realized I needed to let go this part of my self. It had been a wonderful, and very significant part of my life, for some time, and now, that time had passed.

Similarly, and also after much thought, I dispensed with the vast majority of my theological library, hundreds and hundreds of books collected over the better part of my life. This was not simply a matter of getting rid of bound bunches of paper with words printed on them. It was more like saying goodbye to a friend, letting go another part of myself, an integral part of myself, one that was the thinker, avid reader, and lover of ideas. Yet, if I was being honest with myself, I was tired of thinking. Learning was a springtime giving way now to a new season. I felt increasingly pulled into a time of unlearning. So, I rid myself of the books and committed myself to reading very little. The clearing was deeply symbolic, and fantastically refreshing.

Before long, through this process of emptying, I began to harbor a secret suspicion, secret most days even to myself: I was arriving at the edge of an abyss, one I dared not name or even think much about at the time, an unthinkable place I did not want to acknowledge could exist, a place without God. As I drove through the streets of Ramona on my way to the church that morning, reflecting on these things, I began a conversation with God there in the confessional of my car. It was still quite dark out, and the enclosure of the night and warmth from the heater in the cabin of my vehicle made me feel safe. "I am concerned," I whispered with tears soon welling up in my eyes. I could barely bring myself to the next words, though I knew what they were. "I am concerned," I said, "about disengaging with you." Emptying myself over the past few years had been a strange yet tremendously liberating experience, in response to a secret sense of calling, one that my heart knew better than my head. But emptying myself of God, too? I began to wonder. Was that possible? Was that even desirable? "What would that mean?" I asked aloud there in the darkness, not expecting an answer.

An answer came, from a voice that was not my own, "Something good."

Clearer than I even wanted to hear, that's what I heard. "Something good." The words were delicate, and friendly, like an invitation from someone you had known and trusted your entire life. The words at once startled and settled me. After that morning, I would end up burying those words for the better part of a year.

I did not forget the words. How could I? But I could not bring myself to even begin teasing out the possibilities of the consequences of those words. Not at first. The words were too big and too much. I knew actually listening to the words, feeling them out and following them, would lead me to a place I was not ready to go. Everything would change.

When I did finally bring myself back around to reflecting on the experience, I felt its seriousness and knottedness in more ways than one. The Bible refers to what I heard as that "still, small voice."[3] But a word from God, purportedly, is not necessarily a normal experience even for people of faith. For those who pray it is quite natural to wonder where the line is between the voice in your own head and that "other" voice. Actual prayer is dynamic, and what you find yourself saying or hearing in prayer is never a matter of absolute clarity or certainty. That's what makes faith, faith. Spontaneity and surprise, the sublime and the subliminal, are indelible marks of this mystical terrain. In gradually reflecting on my experience in prayer that morning, I found difficulty not only in beginning to own the realization *that* something had happened, something I could not ignore any longer, but there was also difficulty in what appeared to be the contradictory content of this divine conversation. I heard God, telling me to leave God, and that something good nonetheless would come from disengaging with the construct of religious belief that had come to define the very essence of my life. That flew in the face of pretty much the entire Bible, a book encouraging us not to leave God but to seek God. It felt like madness. Would God really ask someone to let go of God?

As a diversion it was tempting to think that perhaps all of this was just in my head. Maybe nothing happened. Nothing beyond what I imagined. Maybe I lost my marbles for a minute. Maybe I was delusional, temporarily, as the result of something disagreeable I had for dinner the evening before. That would certainly be a simpler explanation than a supernatural one, and isn't Ockham's razor—all things being equal the simplest explanation is often the right one—a fair enough rule to apply here?

Hearing voices beyond normal sense perception is clearly a business at least bordering on madness. Such events claim an auditory experience, and sometimes other sensory experiences, in the real world of something or someone other from beyond the realm

3. 1 Kgs 19:12

of the sensory world. How does that even happen? How would something so other touch us who are radically other to that other, and if it did happen, how would we know because of the gulf of otherness?

It is worth pointing out how religious experiences, despite such questions, lie at the very heart of the spiritual life. If not directly for every individual then indirectly by way of the adherents' ties to the founders of their religion. Ramadan for Muslims commemorates Muhammad's first experience of God, revealing the Qur'an. The Bahai Faith traces its origins back to Baha'u'llah and his multiple experiences of the divine. Buddhism, though largely non-theistic, traces its origins to the religious experience of Gautama, a prince of ancient India who after wandering outside the comforts of his palace is so struck by the suffering of the world he is led on a journey of self-discovery culminating in enlightenment.

These are significant claims we find at the center of religions, claims affecting millions and millions of people the world over. How are we to regard those claiming such experiences? If these experiences actually happened it seems remarkable, and, on the other hand, if they did not happen, those claiming the experiences flirt with delusion, self-deception, and madness. We can be polite about our differences of opinion on this sensitive subject, and politeness is important. But at the end of the day how we regard such grandiose claims is also a matter of deciding truth, of what is real versus what is imagined, a matter of what is sane, and what is not. Clearly your interpretation of such religious claims will hinge on what you believe about the world. If you believe the world is a place where God moves, then those not perceiving the divine are more likely to be viewed as the crazy ones, literally those who are out of touch with reality. If you believe the world is devoid of the divine, however, because God is mere wishful thinking for those unable to cope with the harsh realities of life, then, hearing voices might be grounds for committal to a Bedlam.

Is madness thus a matter of power? If the majority of those in power believe 'x,' then 'x' will largely determine the distinction in a society between what is normal and what is abnormal, regardless of whether 'x' is true or false. If 'x' turns out to be false, then, the world itself is but an asylum where those that are more mad lock up those that are less, as the seventeenth-century Anabaptist Thomas Tryon once put it. Madness as such is less a definite mental illness, where one hears voices and the like, and more an issue of control, enforced by the majority worldview. In this way the Parisian historian of thought Michel Foucault argued that madness must be understood not as natural fact but as a cultural construct, one navigated by the administrative and credentialed, steeped in xenophobia, playing out a history not of disease and its cures but rather of freedom and control, knowledge and power. It is interesting to note that the drive to institutionalize the insane reached its peak in the mid-twentieth century, when half a million were psychiatrically detained in the United States with another 150,000 detained in the United Kingdom. Could it really be that there were that many people running around mad needing to be locked up? Perhaps, the asylum is nothing more than a convenient place for inconvenient people.[4]

Surely, though, madness is not only an issue of power. It seems there are some mental conditions that do well with some forms of treatment, helping both the mentally ill and the society of which they are a part. A man terrified to urinate for fear he might drown the world, and another man prohibited from most daily activities convinced he is made entirely of glass about to shatter at any moment, both real examples, are no doubt men who might benefit greatly from therapy or medication or some combination of both. Remedies for such abnormal conditions and other forms of madness have varied throughout the centuries, ranging from diet and exercise to travel, music, marriage, and bloodletting.

Beyond madness as power or illness, the philosopher Ludwig Wittgenstein suggested yet another way for us to regard those hearing voices and the like. Madness, at least sometimes, Wittgenstein thought, had more to do with a change of character. Madness in ancient Greek thought was conceived along similar lines, as a profound change or development in a person and at times in a spiritual vein. The word "madness" from the Greek *mania* is closely related to the Greek word *menos* meaning "spirit." This association between

4. Porter, *Madness*, 2–84.

madness and the spiritual in antiquity is no accident, as even Plato, the most rational of philosophers, was quick to point out that there are many kinds of madness and not all are a malady. Some are of the spirit, Plato said, and of the very best sort, a supreme example being the madness of love.[5]

It is not difficult for us to grasp Plato's perspective on madness if we take a moment to recall falling in love for the very first time. There is an overwhelming intensity to the experience. It changes us. I can still recall the first time I fell head over heels in love. I was not even a teenager yet but a girl living in the neighborhood one day caught my eye and raptured my heart. Tiffany was barely aware I existed of course. But that didn't matter. Once love's spell was cast, I was no longer myself. Or maybe I was more myself than ever before. It is hard to say. Either way, falling in love, I began behaving in ways that would have appeared to the disinterested observer as a little bit out there.

I discovered an inspiration to write—all over my bedroom. In the crevices and corners, on the ceiling, around the doorframe, before I knew it my room was covered with cryptic jottings and the ecstatic expression of my lovesick devotion.

I also made a movie. The horror film entitled "Sinister" employed the use of my friends and family as actors, a script I wrote myself after reading a book on screenplay composition, and editing equipment I purchased with savings from my weekly allowance. It wasn't half bad. I even won an award for the film from the local television company in my hometown that year. Why did I make the movie? Tiffany. To confess, I wanted to create something she could star in so that I could have an excuse to be with her more often. It worked. She was my muse, the object of my desire.

I also changed my entire appearance because of Tiffany, though I might blush to admit it. My hairstyle. My clothing. My mannerisms. I needed to give expression to my elation. And I wanted to up my odds of having anything like an actual boyfriend/girlfriend relationship with her as well. Though so much of this sounds like such foolishness now, love had me feeling, thinking,

5. Plato, *Phaedrus*, 210–11.

and acting differently, decidedly, and it was glorious. "The madness of love," Plato observes, "is the greatest of heaven's blessings, and the proof shall be one which the wise will receive, and the witling disbelieve."[6]

Madness, a social construct delineated by those in power, an actual illness, a change of character, dangerous, and sometimes the greatest of blessings, for me, at the end of the day, it was nothing more than a convenient diversion to entertain about what happened during my drive to the church that morning, postponing deep down what I already knew: though religious experiences are credible or dubious depending on your point of view, when you have one, let the world call you crazy, it does not matter; revelation changes you.

This was not my only experience of the sort. Though it was one of the most significant, others followed, cuing me in to the fact that it was time finally to leave God behind, and first the church. However, and I cannot stress this enough, I do not want to overemphasize these experiences, if that is possible. Such experiences by their nature seem to overstate themselves. Still, revelation aside, more simply, at this time in my life, *something just didn't feel right.* That may sound vague, the opposite of the specificity I experienced in my divine conversation. But the vagueness, the murkiness, the fog, of something not feeling quite right, had a potency at least equal to it.

Similar to how some report their encounters with an apparition, rather than being a stark, overpowering experience, my sense that something was not quite right was just that; a sense, a specter, a hinting. When you have just a sense of something, it is easy to ignore. Our attention tends to gravitate more readily to the loud and ostentatious displays of our experience. Yet many of the finer realities that would illuminate our awareness lack luster. Like a good friend these finer realities prefer to softly tap us on the shoulder, gently encouraging us to turn around, if we will, to notice something that perhaps we have been neglecting for far too long. I once heard the poet David Whyte say that being human means

6. Plato, *Phaedrus*, 210–11.

feeling slightly out of it, most of the time, having a sense that things are somehow off. This sense permeates our lives. It is no respecter of persons. Whereas Christians are sometimes apt to think that the spiritual path means the erasure of our "offness," discomforts, uneasiness, and awkwardness, actually, feeling slightly out of it is a core human competence. You know you're not hiding behind pretense in your own life if you feel slightly out of it, a little bit off, most of the time. It's called being human.

Some of the most honest people with the best minds have understood all too well that you will never feel quite at home in your own life, and you're not supposed to, because your sense of compassion for others depends on your ability to hold within yourself the uneasiness of life. Your compassion for others increases as you are able to embrace the uneasiness within yourself, because you see it is the very same in your neighbor, thus calling forth from you a helping hand and kind words according to the wisdom of your own way.

Paul the Apostle used the image of living in a tent to describe this uneasiness of life.[7] A tent of course is a temporary dwelling. It is something you use when you are in transition from one place to another, when you are not quite settled, externally, but also at times very much internally. The biblical image of the tent highlights the fact that to exist is to be unsettled.

The author of the New Testament book of Hebrews put a slightly different spin on this reality, saying that here, in this life, we do not have anything enduring.[8] What we have here is transience. Indeed, transience is a force unrelenting leading to our sense of uneasiness in life. My own uneasiness, too, this sense that something just didn't feel right, would not let me go. It was an illness that wished to unravel me, or, perhaps, in some strange way, save me.

7. 2 Cor 5:1
8. Heb 13:14

CHAPTER 3

Déjà Vu and Dreams

People wish to be settled; only as far as they are
unsettled is there any hope for them.

—RALPH WALDO EMERSON, CIRCLES

DÉJÀ VU. IT IS that funny feeling you have experienced something
before, in the exact way you are experiencing it in the present moment, right down to the details, as if from another time or another
life, though you cannot recall having actually had the experience.
Some estimate that as many as 70 percent of us have at least one
such experience during our lifetime. Déjà vu, whether actual or
imagined, is a phenomenon of circularity. We find the experience
curious, potent even yet typically brush it off as quickly as it comes
upon us.

A less exotic but similarly circular phenomenon is that of
coming back around to a point in your life, one you have indeed
experienced before, but now in a new way. A mother raising her
three children who suddenly finds herself pregnant again, will be
a mother again, albeit in a new mode, given the unique collection
of lessons she has learned through the joy, heartbreak, and promise
of parenting her first three children. A man braving the no man's
land of unemployment in the wake of the 2008 financial crisis, who

decades earlier found himself likewise without a job, but now near-
ing retirement, comes back around to the experience of workless-
ness in a new light. The twentieth-century Protestant thinker Karl
Barth used to examine theological themes such as freedom and
love in this type of cyclical manner, returning to key tropes again
and again but with slight adjustments, in order to illuminate deeper
meanings within a concept. To my surprise, toward the end of my
ministry in the church, I realized I was in my own kind of circle. My
growing sense that something wasn't right, that the church and pastoring and even religious belief itself was no longer me, led me back
around to the experience of not knowing who I was, an experience
I thought I had left far behind me in adolescence.

During my senior year of high school I found myself almost
homeless. My parents had warned me that if I ever under any conditions brought any illegal substance into our home I would not
be welcome there. I didn't listen. And I really didn't care. Apathy
had swept over me like a tidal wave during this time in my life,
pulling me under and holding me down in a riptide of resistance
to all that had once seemed worthy of my ambitions. In the course
of a year my life had spiraled downward, my waywardness eventually forcing my parents with their tough love approach to boot me
out of the house, landing me in my new living quarters of a room
I rented from my boss, Bill Snelgrove, owner of the local florist
shop in Windsor, Connecticut where I did flower deliveries in my
hometown. Severely stained, orangish carpets lined the floors of an
old beaten up two-story home that looked like a leftover from the
seventies. My new abode was humble with torn curtains hung over
one small window that had an air conditioning unit jutting out that
worked occasionally, along with a door missing from the closet. I
was in no place to complain about any of it. Bill Snelgrove rented
the room to me for almost nothing.

The benefits of having a bed to sleep in were obvious. The
downside, however, of my new living arrangement was that what
started out as a flirtation with illegal substances was given dangerous room to grow. Smoking cigarettes led to smoking marijuana
which led to drinking which led to eating mushrooms which led to
dropping acid which led to smoking crack cocaine.

DÉJÀ VU AND DREAMS

I remember one particularly low night when I had truly lost myself. "Coke" had become a double entendre, as I found myself sitting in the middle of a rented room that was not my own, in the middle of a mess that was my life, smoking coke through a makeshift pipe I had fashioned out of a can of Coke. I can still recall the foul smell of that small, poorly lit room. The noxious odor was due only in part to my own lack of tidiness. The building was infested with cats, at least fifteen of them that I could count, cats that did not have enough litter boxes to match their numbers and litter boxes that were never emptied enough to match their uses. The stench was not helped any by the aroma creeping from the room next to mine. That room belonged to Mike, another tenant. Mike had been a heroine addict most of his life. He was able to convince good-hearted Bill Snelgrove to give him a job and a place to stay long before I came along. Most of the time Mike stank. His addiction meant that things like showering and personal hygiene and cleaning his room were rarely if ever on his to-do list. One night I tried opening the door to Mike's room to "borrow" a cigarette. But the door would not budge and it was not locked. When I was finally able to move it a few small inches, I looked in and glimpsed an entire room, literally floor to ceiling, consumed by an avalanche of junk, a seeming physical extension of the existential mess that was Mike's life. It is true that quite often the outer expresses the inner. But I had no business calling Mike out on his problems when my own life was rapidly going down the drain. Estranged from my family, and myself, dealing drugs, doing drugs, treating the few friends I had left with negligence and contempt, I wondered that night while smoking crack, tweaking, messing around repeatedly with Nine Inch Nails on a tape player and pacing around in a strange room that was not mine, who had I become?

Feeling angry, and empty, I inhaled a huge hit of coke deep into my lungs. I held it in, and then, knelt down in front of a full-length mirror that was leaning lopsidedly against the wall. Finally exhaling, and kneeling there, prayer like, for some time, as I peered into the reflected pools of my own eyes, I was both surprised and unsurprised by what I saw. I saw nothing.

There are two people in every mirror. The one you see. And the other one. The one you don't want to.[1] The modern day mirror was invented in 1835 by the German chemist Justus von Liebig. Still too often it seems we don't want to look at ourselves, not really. To really look at ourselves requires a steeling and stilling that most of us find terribly difficult to muster. For my part I did not want to see what I saw in the mirror that night. Nor did I want to believe what I saw. Seeing nothing in myself was like looking into a mirror darkly, a phrase I would learn later from the Apostle Paul. "For now we see in a mirror, darkly," Paul writes, "but then face to face."[2] This "then" of seeing clearly face to face is a reference to a future age, when all wrongs will be righted. But the "now" of seeing in a mirror, darkly, this is Paul's reference to the enigma of knowing in the present. The word "darkly" used to describe this present knowing, in the original New Testament Greek of the passage, means just that, literally "enigma," something so dark you cannot see it clearly, or at all. Our seeing and knowing in this life is very much like that, akin to looking into an ancient mirror, which in Paul's time was something often fashioned out of polished bronze, giving a reflection that was dim, darkened, diffused. Looking into the mirror that night I did not recognize the enigma looking back.

Seeing nothing, and being thoroughly unsettled by it, I left. After graduating high school I left Snelgrove's, my family and friends, and found myself in South Carolina. Through the love of my girlfriend at the time, and now wife, Erin, and through the help of a pastor and his church back home, I began reading the Bible and realized I needed to stop what I was doing and the way I was living. Soon, I found myself back in Connecticut, at a charismatic church, repenting, and being born again, as Christians sometimes refer to the experience of saving grace at a pivotal moment in one's journey. I committed myself wholeheartedly to Jesus and I was enthusiastically set on living the Christian life. It seemed like overnight it was out with the old and in with the new. New habits. New thoughts. New ways of relating to others and myself. Instead of wasting my

1. Ewing, *Or Is He Both?*, 1–2.

2. 1 Cor 13:12

time smoking blunts, if I didn't know what to do with myself you might find me picking up trash on the side of the road, doing odds and ends around the house to help my parents, or going for prayer walks around the neighborhood. If I couldn't sleep at night, instead of lighting up a spliff, you could find me buried in a book. I read endlessly about spirituality, mysticism, and theology, book after book, some of them thicker than dictionaries, some as part of my studies in undergraduate and then graduate school and many of these texts gobbled up completely of my own accord. Fast forward two decades, two diplomas, two ordinations in two different denominations, one in the National Association of Congregational Christian Churches and one in the United Church of Christ, and now a family man, and lo and behold, I unexpectedly found myself once again feeling like a stranger in my own life, inflicted as if by a heavy dose of déjà vu.

Having a sturdy sense of self is one of the most stabilizing forces we have, shoring us up, day in and day out. I felt beyond bewildered, therefore, as I began to see quite clearly for myself that the self is never static. We buy into the illusion of something more stable only because of the gradual, steadying flow of time covering our eyes to the great movements transpiring, continually, within us, and all around us. The ground beneath our feet, for instance, feels immovable. It appears unmistakably stable. But the appearance of course is an illusion. At this very moment, we hurl through space at a thousand miles an hour, circling the sun, not fixed at all, but rotating. The solar system itself, along with billions and billions of other solar systems making up our Milky Way Galaxy, are also moving, round and round the center a supermassive black hole. On the smallest level, too, the electrons surrounding the nuclei of atoms that make for the ground beneath our feet and the stars overhead and everything else, are constantly moving, randomly, with the even smaller quarks and strings comprising them vibrating. Everything is unsettled.

So very much of life is not at all what it appears to be, and that so not only with regards to the illusion of stability. When we behold color, the fiery yellow of the sun illuminating the world around us, the sap green of a spruce tree set regally against the changing hues of an alizarin crimson sky, we are inclined to believe color is a constitutive part of the world. This appearance, too, is an illusion. For all the objects we see, there is electromagnetic radiation bouncing off these objects and being captured by our eyes. Our eyes can then decipher millions of variations to this radiation. But it is only inside our brains that any of this becomes color. Though it is hard to believe, color is not a part of objective reality. It's all in our heads.

In a similar way, we might be inclined to believe that something as basic as matter is a common part of life. That much seems obvious, right? The trillions of galaxies around us, the trillion upon trillions of stars and planets making up all those galaxies, the oxygen in our own atmosphere, the plastic in our kitchens, the lithium powering our smartphones, nickel, iron, hydrogen, helium, and more make for the elements, the matter, of the known universe. It appears to be everywhere. Whether in the form of a liquid, solid, gas, or plasma, matter seems like the most common thing in the world. Once again, this is an illusion. Matter actually makes up only 5 percent of the known universe. Five times that amount is an entity called dark matter, which isn't really matter at all, leaving a whopping 70 percent of the universe comprised of an invisible force called dark energy, a non-thing we do not yet understand. Clearly all is not as it seems. Not even close.

So it was in my own life. I appeared to be on the opposite end of a spectrum, once lost and using drugs, now found and living in Christ. But much like the colors we are so convinced are out there in the world, and the ground that seems so settled beneath our feet, I began to see that my sense of self was something of a mirage. My self, far from static, had been shifting, changing, evolving and devolving, collapsing and emerging, ebbing and flowing, and would continue to do so, especially in so far as I allowed myself to belong to this becoming.

There were some external forces helping me to see these shifts in my inner being more clearly. During my last few years in the church, for example, in addition to the successes mentioned earlier, there were challenges as well. A satellite campus for a megachurch was planted just a few blocks away from our congregation that initially siphoned off some of our younger families. We also witnessed more than fifty people leaving the church in a relatively short period of time, about eighteen months, in what felt like a mini exodus. These were not disgruntled churchgoers but people who were moving out of town and out of state, due to the cost of living for some, to be closer to extended family for others, and a variety of other reasons. On top of that, I realized I had completed more than sixty funerals by my eighth year of ministry in Ramona, a testament to the aging nature of our congregation.

Such challenges are part and parcel of ministry in the twenty-first century. If you are smart you accept the good with the bad and, most importantly, keep your eye on the blessings. Thank goodness there were plenty of those. To those moving away and passing away, the church was blessed with a healthy influx of talented, generous, and loving new members year after year. Another blessing I continually enjoyed was that of speaking with people personally about matters of life and death, healing and new beginnings. It felt deeply meaningful to engage others in soulful conversation, remembering as the linguist Wittgenstein once pointed out that words are not just words; words are deeds.[3]

There was something about observing these external factors of advancing and receding in church life that began to shed light on my own developments internally. Advancing church growth or having a successful fundraising campaign naturally felt great, and experiencing periodic recessions in attendance due to a new church in the neighborhood or a sudden spike in church members passing or moving away, likewise, naturally felt less than great. If the phenomenon of increasing and decreasing had been decidedly on one side or the other, I would have felt either intoxicated by the allure of success or demoralized by the perception of failure. That there was more or less a balance, however, afforded me an escape from these extremes and instead allowed me to pay attention to my own deepest yearnings. More than anything, as I continued to heed my growing sense of uneasiness with the religious trappings of ministerial life, and as I began reflecting more seriously on the

---

3. Wittgenstein, *Philosophical Investigations*, 146.

revelation of my divine conversation in the car that night, I realized I was yearning for a new way.

But yearning for a new way will not produce it. Only ending the old way can do that. I could not hold onto the old, all the while declaring I wanted something new. The old will defy, deny, and decry the new. There is only one way to bring in the new. You have to make room for it.[4] That was easier said than done. I had been doing church, and being pastor, for so long, that reluctance toward taking a first step in a new direction was only natural. I knew large parts of my identity that had been joyfully employed for years, parts still rehearsing the old narratives I had become quite comfortable with, would suddenly be out of a job. Perhaps, I experienced reluctance in taking that first courageous step into the unknown because I also disbelieved in the possibility of a new happiness. I was afraid. Stepping into the unknown meant letting go of my self. It meant forsaking a core identity I had believed still myself that in reality was now only a fiction. Yet I knew I could not hold on any longer. My life depended on letting go.

So that's what I did. I let go. One Tuesday morning, I sat down with our church moderator and a few key leaders in the congregation to share the news I would be leaving. I had prayed about the decision. I had also talked about it with my wife Erin who could not have been more supportive. Being a pastor wasn't me. Not anymore. And it is hard to say how I knew that. In Icelandic mythology, there is a word that comes close to capturing this kind of knowing, *innsaei*, literally intuition or "the sea within." It is a way of seeing from within. There is a similar concept in Judaic thought, that of *yada*, a kind of deep knowing, involving the whole person. Whatever words we want to give it, had I denied my intuition, this holistic knowing, I knew I would have been denying my very self, and who can live in the world that way? Lofty religious rules and recommendations about self-denial do not change the fact that we are undeniably selves requiring attention, nurture, cultivation, and care.

---

4. Neale Donald Walsch, Facebook post, July 22, 2014. Retrieved from https://www.facebook.com/NealeDonaldWalsch/photos/a.400017592343.181782.4063 8047343/10152199231662344/?type=3&theater

After informing the church of my departure, I shared the news with our children the following week. I decided to speak with Isabella and Joshua individually so I could address any questions they might have as best I could. Isabella and Joshua had both been raised in the church. They had gone to Sunday School since before they could walk. I could only guess how they might react to this monumental change.

As it happened I shared the news with my son first. Joshua and I were sitting at the kitchen table after dinner one night just the two of us. He had finished gobbling up his three Oreo cookies that he looks forward to getting for dessert most nights, assuming he eats his vegetables, three Oreos he often separates and combines into one oversized, gigundo Oreo. I had not actually planned on speaking with him about my departure on this particular evening. But the climate was perfectly calm in the house and it seemed like an ideal moment to share with him the news, even what felt like good news that I did not want to keep bottled up any longer.

"Josh," I said softly, then pausing, letting him know I had something important to say.

"What?" he said looking back at me wide-eyed.

"I'm leaving the church."

"What? Why?" he replied in disbelief.

I paused again and then continued calmly, wanting to convey to him as much in my tone as in my words that this was going to be okay. "Well. . . God told me to."

"He did?" Joshua asked with the utmost sincerity.

"Yes. He did. The church—it's not me anymore."

"Will we have enough money?" was the very next thing Joshua wanted to know.

My heart sank. No father wants his children worrying about such things. Even at ten-years-old, Joshua had long been something of a pragmatist, like my wife, a quality I admire in both of them, an important counter balance to my sometimes less than pragmatic ways.

"Yes, we'll be fine," I reassured him. "Mommy and I have talked about this at length. She has a new job now after being at home with you and Bella when you were little. Mommy's income will help. Plus, we spend money doing a lot of things we really don't need to do. So we are going to cut back a little and simplify. What's most important is that we have each other. We're all connected. This change is going to be good for me and it's going to be good for our whole family. Mommy and I really believe that."

He thought about this for a moment. Then, casually and cheerfully, Joshua replied, "Okay," and was off to more important things like playing one of his video games.

In retrospect I am not sure exactly what I expected from his response. But the resiliency Joshua demonstrated both that night and in the months ahead genuinely surprised me. Even more than resiliency, it was his nonchalance, his confidence in our family unit, and his trust in me, that this change really would be good for our whole family, that warmed my heart. My twelve-year-old daughter Isabella's response when I shared the news with her later that same evening also surprised me.

"I'm leaving the church," I told Bella during our car ride back home after picking her up from an aerial silks class at the local gymnasium.

"That's great!" she exclaimed.

I was so taken aback by her response that I almost slammed on the brakes. I slowed the car so as to examine her face and what she meant more carefully. But Bella simply peered back at my examination with her beaming countenance, only to say, "What? I'm excited for you!"

"You're excited? Really? Why?" I asked perplexed.

Bella had practically hopped out of her seat at this point to face me more directly. "Because," she said, "you're going to be happier."

I was stunned by her insightfulness though I probably should not have been. Children are deeply perceptive. Bella had known the truth of my unhappy condition apparently for some time. She could see that I needed to take a courageous step toward reclaiming my own happiness even before I could see it. Wittgenstein got it right when he said nothing is so difficult as not deceiving yourself.[5]

---

5. Wittgenstein, *Culture and Value*, 34.

I was deeply moved by the graciousness of my family in supporting my decision to leave the church. That alone meant a lot. Likewise, the church as a whole, though deflated by my announcement, was kind and understanding. I told them the truth, that I felt called to stop, and that what lay ahead for me was unknown. I was leaving on good terms, not running off to a bigger and better opportunity somewhere else, which I heard through the grapevine some had feared, and that, too, helped to ease my exit. I genuinely did not know what I was going to do. I only knew I had to let go and that now was the time. I gave the church three months notice, according to our church bylaws, which allowed for a search committee to secure an interim minister, and, before I knew it, my time in the ministry was over.

Nighttime dawned as fertile space for me soon after my departure. Sleepless nights were couched in quiet reflection. When I did sleep, my dream time was laced with luminosity.

About a month after leaving the church, one night, I dreamt my son and I were sitting on the couch together in our living room. We were watching television. I do not remember what we were watching. What I do distinctly remember is a pleasantly plump Samoan baby seated on the sofa with us. The baby was absolutely adorable and looked to be somewhere between six months and one-year-old. He was sitting there in his diaper, between us, propped up with his back against the soft leather of our espresso-colored couch. The baby was unusually fat. I did not know who he was, and I was not sure what he was doing there. But all three of us seemed rather happy; that is, until the baby started going to the bathroom right then and there on the couch, and number two at that. But Josh and I did not fret. We noticed this beginning to happen, and so I casually picked up the baby, wrapping my two large hands securely underneath his armpits and around his soft, smooth torso, and began walking towards the bathroom at the end of the hallway to take care of the situation. I realized, however, as Joshua following closely behind gave me a sharp glance of concern, we were not going to make it. I took a quick detour and went to the next closest room, the kitchen. I seated the child with his many rolls of baby blubber in the sink, positioning his bottom directly over the drain so he could comfortably and conveniently relieve himself, and relieve himself he did. This baby, whom I did not know nor have the foggiest clue as to why he was hanging out in my living room, with his diaper now tossed aside, proceeded to "let go" in a most massive way, seemingly without end. He was like a faucet, going and going, and the expression on his face as I held him there was one of absolute contentment.

When I awoke, the dream like a vapor quickly began to dissipate, as dreams often do, so I seized upon it by using a kind of trick from the poet and philosopher John O'Donohue. Though it may sound unusual, as we journey through life we can forget who we are, or not notice who we are becoming, and in this way be out of sync with our very own selves. There are few things more dangerous. If ever you find yourself in such a place, deadened by the banality of routine, having misplaced your wonder over the sheer mystery of your own life, taking time to notice your dream life can help. Curiously, it is there in our dream time we find reminders, reflections, and the residue of our passions and fears with the power to awaken us once more. Pausing for a minute before rolling out of bed allows space for the mind to recall our dreams. Some mornings nothing may come to mind at first. You might even believe you did not dream. Surprisingly, however, if you give yourself time when waking for observance of that threshold between the conscious and subconscious, you begin remembering your wildness revealed there in your dreams.

My dream, so vivid, so real, everything utterly familiar in it with the exception of a Samoan child, brought a huge small smile to my face as I lay there in bed musing on it. I could not help but laugh out loud, too, as I thought about the dream's ridiculousness. Erin gave me a queer stare from across the room like I had completely lost it. It had been a month since I left the church, and this dream, like a confirmation, felt utterly and deeply relieving, I imagine not unlike the relief the baby seemed to enjoy by relieving himself in my dream. Perhaps the baby *was* me I wondered, a child within, making an appearance there in my dream life, showing me something I needed to see. In addition to the many blessings of ministry, for years I had also dealt with a lot of crap in the church. Most people in the congregations I served were good-natured. But there were always a few manipulative personalities more interested in power or prestige than in fulfilling the mission of the church. Logistically, too, there were administrative challenges big and small on a near daily basis. Had all of this built up inside of me more than I ever realized? Now that I was no longer in the fray, I was emotionally relieved, and my dream demonstrated this to me vividly and visually.

In the months following my departure from the church, looking at my dreams was like looking into a mirror, lightly, not too seriously or analytically, but simply allowing myself to see and feel the healing that was taking place in my inner life. It is said that Asklepios the Greek god of medicine healed by using dreams. Paying attention to my own dreams, even writing them down for a time, soon became a new practice taking only minutes when I awoke but granting me glimpses of grace, helping me to circle back around to raw panoramas of my interior life.

Another night, about two months after my departure from the church, I dreamt my daughter and I were driving down the highway together through an open field, the sunshine raining down from an enormously clear blue sky above. Isabella and I were seated atop our car, almost as if in a carriage, until we began happily floating up, higher and higher, away from everything, performing tricks for each other among the clouds, laughing uncontrollably and celebrating. Then the dream was over. Upon waking, resting in bed and looking up at the ceiling, I felt free. Leaving had produced levity.

In our dreams, the strange, thrilling, terrifying, and exotic remind us that our lives are a tremendous place of vision and becoming. Observance of our dream life does not need to be intrusive or overly interpretive. Observance itself has considerable power. Rather than searching for the meaning of a dream, we can learn much about ourselves simply by observing our thoughts, feelings, and memories surfacing in our dream time as symptoms of the soul. Dreams, in this way, provide a less censored view of our internal landscape than conscious self-analysis.[6] Learning to gently observe, and then write down, images, feelings, and thoughts from our dreamscape, as another form of Examen, gives us a way of

6. Moore, *Care of the Soul*, 4–13, 134.

looking into the heart of our lives. For a period, when I was young, I remember how much I thoroughly enjoyed observing people as a pastime. When I did not have much else to do, I would watch others, in the park or at the mall, walking, talking, busy with the activities of everyday life. Now it was a joy to rediscover the practice of observance in my dream time. Whereas the practice of observance earlier in my life had been externally focused, this new internal viewing or in-sight brought about just that, insight, into the condition of my soul. My condition it seems was marbled.

My dreams revealed light but also darkness. One night I dreamt I was in a cave. There, before me in the cave, was a shimmering stream of water. I was preparing to jump the stream which, while beautiful, appeared to be an obstacle on my journey through the cave. I realized I would need a running start. It was going to be a close call but I felt some assurance I would make the jump. Erin was with me in the cave, just to my right, and I think our children as well just to her right, though it was hard to tell for the incandescent lighting. A small fire burned behind us in the cave, casting beautiful shades of gold and gray upon the cave walls with a flurry of shadows. The air would have been dank were it not for the warmth of the fire. Looking intently at the water before me, I began backing up a few paces, as much as I could, gauging the distance I would need to jump and eyeing a few good spots from which to launch myself. Before I could begin my dash, however, there suddenly appeared from the darkness above an exceptionally enormous bat. The wingspan of the creature must have been eight feet or more. I marveled at the creature, and then found myself dodging left and right, trying to shield myself from its attempts to mount my back. It wanted to lift me up. The more I tried to shoo it away, the more it persisted, furiously, with razor-sharp talons. Then I awoke. The dream was so rife with symbols I could not resist doing some research.

Bats are elemental creatures. In terms of their imagery, in Jungian psychology, bats are an archetype of death. Caves, on the other hand, a form of containment, are typically a womb symbol, a transitional space representing the potential for life.[7] It was in-

---

7. Stevens, *Ariadne's Clue*, 104–5, 367.

teresting to notice how my dream in this way contained elements of both life and death. As I turned the dream over in my mind, the cave reminded me of how Gautama, the Buddha, would meditate in caves, and how the first verses of the Qur'an came to Muhammad in a cave, and how Jesus was born in a cave, and then born again when he rose from the dead in a cave.[8] The antagonizing figure of the bat in my dream I realized represented my experience of death and dying in leaving the church, but also something else. The bat with its huge wingspan represented a colleague who had tried to "lift me up" at lunch the day before.

Once it was known that I was leaving the church, people approached me both out of concern and curiosity. Leaving, without any specificity about where I was heading, or what I was going to be doing, naturally enough appeared alarming to some, despite my reassurances that this was a good and necessary move for me. As I sat down to talk with people one after another, quelling concerns, conveying with my countenance as much as with my words that everything, really, was going to be alright, I noticed on more than one occasion I felt poked, prodded, and even paralyzed by the mixed motives of some who, rather than seeking consolation for themselves or offering an affirmation of my new journey, seemed to have other agendas, and I came away wounded from these conversations.

My lunch with Eric, a fellow minister, precipitating my dream later that night, was one such conversation. When he called I was not sure exactly why he wanted to get together. "I've just been thinking about you," he told me. That sounded innocent enough. Still, we had only done lunch one other time over the past eight years, which made me hesitant of the invitation. After mulling it over, I decided against my better judgment to say yes to meeting up. Through my years in the ministry I had very much become a yes-man out of a desire to serve people pastorally in whatever capacity they needed me, to be there for them, regardless of whether or not it was in my best interest, and this proved a hard habit to break.

Eric and I met for lunch at Marie Callender's on a Tuesday. As he chomped away on a sandwich and salad I leisurely sipped on a

---

8. Taylor, *Learning to Walk in the Dark*, 127–28.

cup of coffee. The banter was light at first. But it became clear about halfway through our meal that the meeting was not agenda free. Eric informed me of a new coaching program he was excited about that our religious denomination had recently embraced as part of a new initiative passed at one of our conferences. This was at least the third time I had been hit with information about the program. But I was not interested in hearing about initiatives and programs. I felt raw coming to lunch that day, and candidly told Eric as much first thing as we sat down. I had left behind the familiar grounds of ministry, the church, and my pastoral identity only a couple months earlier, which Eric knew, and I told him how difficult it was deciding just to come out to lunch. The dis-ease was written all over my face. But none of this seemed to matter. It was clear by the end of our conversation that at least one of the reasons, maybe even the real reason, for getting together was so that Eric could plant a seed for the new coaching program. As we talked, it surfaced that Eric was looking to promote the program not only for the denomination but also as a potential new source of income for himself. He was feeling me out, as a prospective client, a recipient for his would be services.

I do believe the intentions behind Eric's words were good, and I fully acknowledge I may have been in such a place emotionally as to misinterpret some of what I think I heard. In between what I want to say, what I try to say, and what I actually say, what you want to hear, what you think you hear, and what you actually hear, there are at least nine possibilities for misunderstanding. Emotions aside, communication, perception, and interpretation are thickly textured terrains. I know Eric well enough to know he is a helper to his core. But what I felt from him that day, especially after cueing him in to my unsettled condition, hurt. I felt used. What wounded me the most, however, was not the interaction. It was the realization afterwards that sitting there across from me at our dining table all along I had been looking at myself.

This was not the first time I had entertained the possibility that maybe, in my own ministry with others, I had at times come with an agenda beyond simply helping another. After my lunch with Eric, the more I thought about it, the more this possibility seemed to be the reality. The revelation cut deep, and the deeper it went the more clearly I saw my own failure to be there more fully for others in the past. I remembered how many times I sat down with people, at my office or a coffee shop, not only to love them or help them or serve them in some way unique to their situations, but also to invite them to become a church member or find out if they had been baptized or with an eye toward increasing their Sunday attendance. The justification for this in my mind was that I was killing two birds with one stone. Why not help someone going through a marital crisis, say, and, at the same time, lay the groundwork for a potential new member, new giver, and new Sunday worshipper? This way of approaching people, dually, was easy to rationalize, and crept into me over the years because as a pastor I was not only in the position of being a counselor, teacher, and servant, I was also the head of an organization requiring an abundance of volunteers and ample resources to accomplish its mission. I do not want to sound like something I was not. I was not a shark. Yet too often it was easy to overlay objectives, bringing other agendas to the table when meeting with those who really just wanted someone to care for them, to listen to them, to simply be with them. Now, being on the other side of the table myself, raw, and in need of nothing more than a compassionate presence with few words, big ears, and an even bigger heart, I could see how misplaced my motives were at times, and how my "good intentions" to grow the church might have made those in need feel worse rather than better.

I am not sure why but one day while driving, not long after my departure from the church, I began to wonder how I had become so focused on the agenda of church growth. Go to just about any ecclesial conference or ministerial gathering and if you eaves drop on a conversation or two you are bound to hear plenty of numbers thrown around. This many people saved. This many people served. This many new worshippers. This many new members. This many baptized. This much raised. This much donated. On and on. When I first began serving in the church, however, fresh out of divinity school and straight into the ministry, for my first three years of service, for the life of me I could not recall having any preoccupation with church numbers, statistics, growth, or development at all. This surprised me. I had almost completely forgotten a very different mindset. Instead of an obsession with numbers, aimed at growing the church, I had other passions.

Back in the day I had been enthralled with insights I had come across in studying philosophy, theology, and church history, ideas of real relevance and more than one might imagine from simply glancing at a pile of dusty books in a university library. Ideas are powerful. It is funny, though, how things, rather than ideas, so often are what catch our attention in an age of technology and consumerism. Yet the really interesting things are not things at all but ideas. Most any *thing* you can think of, in fact, began as an idea. Your smartphone. Your washing machine. Your computer. Your car. Forks, spoons, and knives. Hammers, drills, and screwdrivers. Pistons, pulleys, and engines. Even those natural objects in the world we had no hand in fashioning ourselves were, from a theological vantage point, originally ideas in the mind of God before finding form through the gift of creation. Ideas one might say are the original root of everything. From the idea that the sun rather than the earth is the center of our solar system, to the idea that your sexual orientation or skin color should matter no more than the color of your eyes, though intangible and invisible ideas have been known to change the world.

In addition to my love of ideas early in ministry, I remembered I was also passionate about writing, to the extent that Erin would poke fun at me during our newlywed years when some mornings she would learn I had been awake most of the night, my insomnia eventually cured yet again by spending several hours hacking away at a keyboard, composing something for no one, given I was finished with school and no longer had a reason to write. No formal reason that is. But write I did. I couldn't help myself. In writing, I felt in touch with my true self. There was something transformative and transgressive about language that I loved, and this eventually led to the joy I found in speaking from the pulpit. Speaking and writing, I discovered, were ways for me to be me, while at the same time giving myself away to others.

What had happened? At one point, church numbers had not mattered to me one iota. Then, voila, so many of my efforts and so much of my energy were being devoted to the success of growing the church. I felt puzzled. As I thought about it, I remembered my first pastoral position in a large church, and a new emphasis I encountered there. At our weekly staff meeting, two of the three senior ministers who were also my mentors led all the staff through the attendance roster religiously, hemming and hawing and scrutinizing the numbers as well as the reasons for any significant variance in attendance, encouraging us to celebrate our climb toward an ever greater worship presence in the community. I have to admit that their enthusiasm was positively contagious. Or was it infectious? Either way, I did not question the mindset. The theological reason behind this emphasis on growth seemed to be Matthew 28. Here Jesus commissions his disciples to go and make disciples of all nations. Christians famously refer to the passage as the Great Commission. It is ironic, though, that Jesus himself never calls the commission great. What he does call great is the command to love, elsewhere in Matthew 22. It is the call to love, not convert, that Jesus considers greater than anything. Still, the so-called Great Commission seems to be the driving force in many churches today.

Why had I become so focused on the dream of making disciples, making the attendance increase, and making the cogs of the institution turn? Indeed, the very idea of "making" things happen in church life felt less natural and more mechanical the more I thought about it. A reason I had given myself in the past for this growth mindset was that numbers are people. When you increase the numbers in worship, you increase the people who might have their lives changed by the presence of God moving through the music, the message, and the fellowship. Makes sense. The problem was the mission of making disciples had never really been *my* mission. Yes, there was excitement in contributing to a thriving organization. But numbers had never been my true passion, even numbers for the kingdom. I was now beginning to remember that, and the more I remembered the more I felt an invitation to the wellspring of that remembrance, seeing once again with fresh eyes who I was, what really mattered to me, and what did not.

CHAPTER 4

Neurosis, Nemesis, Happiness

I had been given so many formulas for happiness,
systems of life, and religions that nothing of the sort
moved me any longer.

—ALBERT CAMUS, *INTUITIONS*

ON THE AFTERNOON OF November 14th 1940, Winston Churchill was handed a startling piece of news. A German radio signal had been secretly intercepted. According to the transmission, the Germans were planning a bombing raid on the town of Coventry later that very night. The raid was to be retaliation for a recent attack on Munich. The Germans planned to absolutely annihilate their target. Churchill knew there was plenty of time to warn and safely evacuate the people in the city. Instead of saving them, however, what did Churchill do? He did nothing.

Historical records educate us as to why Churchill made such a seemingly mad move.[1] Earlier that year, an Enigma decryption machine had been recovered by British Intelligence from a sunken U boat, enabling them to decipher the top secret German code known as Ultra. This gave the British unbridled access to all vital communications happening through German military radio traffic.

1. Jenkins, *Inhumans*, 10.

48

Every plan of the German high command was compromised. Yet Hitler's staff remained in the dark. By evacuating Coventry, Churchill would expose the fact they had deciphered Ultra, thus forfeiting this critical intel for all future missions. Churchill was put in the position of deciding the fate of thousands. With great remorse, he decided the code was too valuable to risk. In order to help win the war, Churchill allowed the people of Coventry to burn that night, while he sat safely back in London, doing nothing.

It has been said that the only thing necessary for the triumph of evil is for good men to do nothing. But that is wrong. At best it is a half-truth. Churchill's course of action, or rather inaction, surely incites divided opinions. But it also reminds us of another side to nothing, an instrumental side, a valuable and virtuous side. Even in the smallest of scenarios we sometimes fail to notice its fecundity. In the midst of a family squabble, holding your tongue and saying nothing, to stop the downward spiral, as a first step toward peace, is sometimes the best move. In a heated argument with a co-worker, taking a time out to absent yourself from the situation, calm down, and reacquire a better perspective can be the way forward. Absence and nothingness are not always a source of villainy. For Churchill one can make a strong case that doing nothing, in fact, was a sacrifice of the highest order, not for the triumph of evil but of good. His choice of nothing makes us uncomfortable nonetheless.

The larger idea of nothingness does not sit so well with us either. We would rather do just about anything, even the mundane of paying the bills or cleaning out the cat's litter box, rather than risk the nothingness of simply being; alone, in silence, inactive and undistracted. Why is that? Are we that unfamiliar with being? Do we think of being as that strange? Putting aside for the moment our obsession with activity, our altruistic justifications for activity, and the risk of boredom with inactivity, there also seems to be a level of real anxiety when it comes to being rather than doing, nothing over something. Yet approaching the nothingness of being lies at the heart of being human. "I need not be afraid of the void," Michael Novak encourages us in his book *The Experience of Nothingness*. "The void is part of my person. I need to enter consciously into it. To try to escape from it is to live a lie. It is also to cease to be.

My acceptance of my despair and emptiness constitutes my being; to have the courage to accept despair is to be."[2] Being is difficult. It requires a commitment to honesty, courage, recognition of how widespread the experience of nothingness is, as well as a willingness to see, approach, and honor the void in your own life.[3]

The experience of nothingness played an important role in my own journey. Soon after leaving the church behind, I began leaving God behind, though I noticed the dissipation of the divine was less an intentional activity and more an allowance to move into nothingness. I stopped reading the Bible. I stopped praying. I discontinued my meditation routines. Even my self-talk about God, which had become second nature over the years, I allowed to fade into nothingness. Through this process I would catch myself, late at night sometimes, out of habit, thinking about God or starting to talk to God, and I would stop, making room instead for the emptiness. But leaving God behind was not as simple as no longer opening Scripture or folding my hands and bowing my head. As when there is a death, or a divorce, though the trappings of a relationship may come quickly to a halt, there remains a trace of presence, lingering, a haunting of what once was nearly impossible to erase.

My letting go of God was not exactly like the death of God. God had been the underlying impetus for letting go. In a peculiar way, God was now diffused, a kind of barely perceptible background radiation. The letting go of God was also not exactly like a great divorce. I was not once a theist, now an atheist, separated from my former Partner. The closest analogy I can think of to describe the experience is that of the German philosopher Martin Heidegger who in the early twentieth century originally had a strong religious outlook, until the devastations of the First World War left him and others feeling as though faith in any sort of benevolent deity was untenable at best and irresponsible at worst. Yet when Heidegger eventually abandoned his faith in 1919 it did not translate into simple atheism. Heidegger's outlook continued to be deeply spiritual, throughout his life, though his way of phrasing and approaching

2. Novak, *The Experience of Nothingness*, 67.
3. Novak, *The Experience of Nothingness*, ix–xxiv.

life's questions shifted noticeably. My letting go of God came about not as the result of a devastating world war as it did for Heidegger but from something much more tacit, a sense of uneasiness, one that extended beyond the uneasiness which is part and parcel of being human, one that had more to do with the disjointed nature of who I was becoming, a pastor who did not believe that God is real in any substantial sense of the word, feeling spiritual yet not spiritual and without new language to talk about it. That may sound incoherent: how can you be spiritual yet not spiritual? But people are bundles of contradictions, with coherence often being an idea we superimpose on the supremely less tidy reality that is the self. Howard Jacobson got it right when he said whoever lusts after coherence lusts after lies.[4]

The vacuous nature of my new dwelling outside the church, detached from religious devotions, without God, gave way to an uncomfortable surge in self-consciousness. Admittedly, I have always been somewhat self-consciousness, more so than others, I think. One can never be too sure, and the more one thinks about it the more suspicious one becomes of a neurosis. Nevertheless, the sudden combination of having no full-time work, minimal social interactions, deep uncertainty about what the future held, as well as feeling for the first time the existential fault lines of no longer knowing God as the centerpiece of my identity, quickly resulted in a squirmishness making it difficult just to be in my own skin. I often felt like my greatest enemy.

What helped just a little and just enough was moving. I would walk for miles most days, wandering through the neighborhoods and mountains where I live and secretly burrowing through the busy city streets of San Diego. There was something soothing about moving. Moving my body gave stillness to my being. I did not really understand why. Nor did I feel like I had to understand. My mind was tired, and simply noticing the vitality of the connection between motion and being was healing. Moving was a way of remembering and reconnecting with myself. "I move, therefore I

---

4. Jacobson, *The Dog's Last Walk*, 66.

am,"[5] writes Haruki Murakami, a play on Rene Descartes' famous *cogito ergo sum*, "I think, therefore I am," though Murakami strikes a chord closer to my own sense of being at the time. Locomotion has a way of lubricating the dark, broken faculties of the mind as it anchors our being deeper in the raw simplicity of nature's ever shifting reality.

Walking in nature I found room to clear my mind, while walking in the city I found a way for my searing self-consciousness to be present with people, albeit at a safe distance, walking in the midst of others while never really interacting with others, present and absent at the same time. I later learned that one of my favorite authors after becoming a Christian, the Danish theologian Soren Kierkegaard, operated in a similar way. Kierkegaard loved to walk the streets of Copenhagen. Throughout his life he had many acquaintances, yet rarely anyone he could call a friend, seldom ever having guests to his own residence. Kierkegaard was somewhat of a loner, the individualist, feeling more at home in social isolation where his chafing self-consciousness would be minimized. Yet, according to one of his nieces, he seemed to find daily pleasure in walking, wandering the streets of Copenhagen where he would cross paths with those who knew him well enough, and with whom he would converse briefly enough. "It was a way to be among people for a man who could not be with them, a way to bask in the faint human warmth of brief encounters, acquaintances' greetings, and overheard conversations. A lone walker is both present and detached from the world around, more than an audience but less than a participant. Walking assuages or legitimizes this alienation."[6] In my own wandering I discovered modulation for my alienation.

It is interesting that the word "wander" comes from the verb "to wind" and is related to the German word *wandeln* meaning "to change." The wanderer does not find change a threat. Change is understood as an invitation to possibility.[7] Allowing for space and time in your own life to wander can actually bring you into a deeper

5. Murakami, *1Q84*, 29.

6. Solnit, *Wanderlust*, 23–26.

7. O'Donohue, *Eternal Echoes*, 46.

rhythm with yourself. In a world swarming with a superabundance of adages and advice you can unknowingly become tone-deaf to your own wisdom. Part of the terror then is to take back your own listening, to hear your own voice, for we cannot live very long in a world that is interpreted for us.[8] I had learned the hard way that our age is retrospective, as Ralph Waldo Emerson observed in the nineteenth century, though his remarks are just as applicable today. Our age "builds the sepulchers of the fathers. It writes biographies, histories, and criticism. The foregoing generations beheld God and nature face to face; we, through their eyes. Why should not we also enjoy an original relation to the universe? Why should not we have a poetry and philosophy of insight and not of tradition, and a religion by revelation to us, and not the history of theirs?"[9] As an author it seems Emerson paradoxically held a reverence for words and recommended their rejection. He could not help but write his ideas while at the same time sharing the caveat not to heed his insights too much rather than looking to your own.

Over the years I had entertained so many insights from others, interpretations of life, and formulas for happiness that I actually lost touch with the wisdom of my own way. Shutting down those other voices, even the voice of God, and enjoying the simplicity of moving, helped attune my hearing inward once again. In walking I experienced a return to my own nature. Not only were the demons of the past exorcised more readily. There was also a freedom to think on those things that were truly precious to me, or to think on nothing at all. Henry David Thoreau, who is said to have walked four hours a day or more, through hills, fields, and woods, recommended walking like a camel, "which is said to be the only beast which ruminates when walking."[10] Apparently the patriarch Isaac, son of Abraham, thought the same. "Isaac went out in the evening to walk in the field . . ." the Bible tells us.[11] The Hebrew word translated in the verse as "walk" is curiously a term of ambiguous

8. Hildegard of Bingen, "Speaking to the Soul," para. 1.

9. Emerson, *Nature*, 9.

10. Thoreau, *Walking*, 247.

11. Gen 24:63

meaning, equally translatable as "meditate," suggesting a kinship between movement and meditation, musing and meandering, the mind set free as we freely traverse nature's paths known and unknown. The verse concludes noting that Isaac looked up and saw those meditative creatures, camels, approaching in the distance.

As my meditations drifted ever farther away from God, I noticed something important about God that struck me as both obvious and funny: God is a word. God is a word just as tree is a word. At this very moment, in fact, as I write, I am situated in front of a tree, wonderfully wild, branches sprawling, limbs contorting, its deep emerald leaves interspersed with lightly colored patches of new growth. I do not happen to know the name of this type of tree. And I do not need to know its name. Name or no name, I notice just how stunning the tree is in its own right. When I talk about the tree, as I am doing here, when I say the word "tree" referring to this tree, I know the word is not the same as its referent, the actual tree that beckons for me to stop writing and thinking and to simply enjoy its allure, the coarse bourbon-colored bark and gentle rays of sunshine illuminating parts while casting shadows round others. The tree is beautiful. If I were to mistake the word tree for the tree itself I would be committing a true crime. T—R—E—E does not equal what my eyes behold. Why, then, I wonder, when so many of us talk about God, do we not only seem to casually forget that God is a word, minimally, but furthermore, we seem to assume this strong identification between the word and whatever it is that word actually refers to as though asserting the word somehow assures a reality? The very moment we begin to speak or think or write about "God" we have already gone far, far off the path of actually articulating anything closely resembling the One to whom we hope our language refers. The limit of language is revealed by it being impossible to describe that which corresponds to a sentence, without simply repeating some version of the sentence, or without leaving language, and pointing here, look, this is the thing I am talking about.[12] If there is already an obvious gap between the word tree, and the actual beauty of the tree in front of me, how much greater

12. Wittgenstein, *Culture and Value*, 10.

and wider and deeper the difference and distance between G—O—D and that which we perhaps dare not speak of? To speak of God will irrevocably create an idol. Indication is idolatry. The Chinese sage Lao Tzu once settled a dispute among his disciples regarding this very issue. His disciples were arguing about one of the master's teachings, that the one who knows does not speak, and the one who speaks does not know. After some debate, the disciples decided to ask Lao Tzu about the meaning of the teaching. Sitting outside, looking around, Lao Tzu said, "Which of you knows the fragrance of a rose?" They each nodded, yes, they all knew the fragrance of a rose. "Now," Lao Tzu said, "put it into words." They all fell silent.

Ask a hundred people what they mean when talking about God and you might very well get a hundred different answers. If you are not referring to some long-bearded male figure sitting on a throne in the clouds but instead to, say, "that than which nothing greater can be conceived," to borrow a phrase from Saint Anselm of Canterbury, the highest Good, the greatest Beauty, the most perfectly conceived notion of Truth, and so on, it seems inevitable language will always fall short. This semantic shortfall is compounded by the fact that many words, in any language, over time, experience what linguists call semantic drift when the meanings of words change. Take the old Jack Benny radio show for example. Phil Harris, the leader of the band on the show, a kind of randy fellow, at one point on one of the programs is talking to his wife, Alice Faye, and says, "Come on, baby! Admit it! No one makes love better than me!" To our ears, this sounds a bit shocking, like a reference to something rather intimate you would not expect to hear on a national radio program, or at least not in the 1940s. But this would be to misunderstand the actual meaning here. As late as the 1940s "make love" meant just kissing, or perhaps dropping your handkerchief in front of someone and coming on to them, not sexual intercourse. The meaning of "make love" has changed, gradually, over the years, a process confounding the overly neat and packaged idea we have about words embodying a static meaning with a consistent referent. In truth, our words are far from stable, drifting over time and in different directions. Language is messy.[13] A word like God will mean one thing to a Muslim, and another to a Jew, and yet another to a Christian, and that so differently to different Muslims, Jews, and Christians, and differently at different points in time, and place, according to ever evolving, shifting patterns in language and meaning.

For as long as I can remember as a Christian I had always implicitly acknowledged the problem of religious language, with variance of meanings, and the question of how our God-talk could possibly reach across the chasm to the impossibly other referent of our discourse. In actual practice, however, I typically gave these realities little more than lip service, continuing to talk freely and frequently about God, and not thinking too much of it. That changed.

During my last few years in the church, whether preaching on Sundays or discussing matters of faith one-on-one with parishioners, I had an increasing lack of confidence conversationally when speaking with others about God that we were intending or meaning the same thing. Too often others' discourse about God seemed to embody assumptions about who God is and how God operates I no longer shared. I did not think one way of talking about God was now necessarily better than another because I did not know if I had any new meaning to attach to the word. What came as a huge relief after leaving the church was finally abandoning language about God. The conversations I then enjoyed instead, to my surprise, were conversations with strangers sitting in the backseat of my car.

Not knowing what I wanted to do after pastoring, quite practically I needed a paycheck to supplement Erin's income so that after the financial sacrifices we agreed to make in allowing for me to leave the church, we could at least break even each month, hopefully. Driving for Uber and Lyft came as a no-brainer. Rideshare driving does not require any training. All you need is a driver's license, a decent vehicle, and a background check. But I also liked the idea of "Ubering" because I yearned to do something absolutely basic having just finished with the intricacies of full-time ministry. Driving people from point A to point B, with the flexibility to be

13. McWhorter, *The Story of Human Language*, 23.

my own boss and the freedom to determine my own hours, working around school schedules for Isabella and Joshua and tending to more of the cooking and cleaning around the house was a great fit. It also seemed to be a fulfillment of prophecy.

Eons ago, when I was in my middle school, students in social studies were required to take an assessment that would indicate professions likely to suit your personality. When we received the results back after lunch one afternoon, the number one recommendation on my assessment was taxi driver. "Taxi driver?" I remember thinking to myself with horror and disbelief. Why would they even include that as an option? Were they trying to demoralize some of us? Were they simply laying out as many options as possible beyond some of our aspirations to be an astronaut or President of the United States? Whatever the reason, I noticed many of my friends had suggestions like nurse, lawyer, teacher, accountant, beautician, engineer. No one else to my knowledge had taxi driver. No one. Yet here I was decades later fulfilling the written word.

The human psyche is a complex of competing claims, a constellation of identities not always agreeing, pushing and pulling on one another, and though at first my pastoral, professional, and highly productive selves felt beyond humbled at my transition from the church to chauffeur, my larger sense of self actually welcomed the change. It was an opportunity for simplicity, rest, and rumination. Driving, round and round the streets of San Diego, was akin to the catharsis of walking. The added element of open-ended conversation, talking regularly with a fascinating and diverse array of people, allowed me to touch, and be touched, by real difference. There was deep honesty in discussing anything from politics to the environment to family dynamics to holistic healthcare and beyond, I imagine almost like spilling your guts to that anonymous bartender who also happens to play the role of a pseudo psychiatrist. I appreciated the candor that seemed to naturally color the majority of my conversations with passengers, rooted perhaps in a shared assumption that we would most likely never see each other again, so, why not speak your mind. The work felt almost playful. Whenever it came up in a conversation that I was a former pastor—which either inspired curiosity and a flurry of questions, or awkward silence for the remainder of the fare—I discovered a rare opportunity, on days when I had the courage, to begin, barely, teasing out a narrative of what had happened to me in religion, who I was, and who I was becoming.

Eastern wisdom has been known to recommend work, simple, basic forms of work, as a medicine for our malaise. Sweeping the patio. Doing the dishes. Repairing something broken. These activities have a way of drawing us out of the mind, massaging us with motion, making room in the heart for healing. Driving, often with the windows down, the wind blowing, sun caressing, traversing the same roads in a virtual circle, again and again, before returning to my same point of departure, home, yet never quite the same, conversing with a plethora of people, I noticed I felt happy.

Each new day brought me in contact with someone new. Where conversations moved beyond the shallow end to the deep, driver and passenger graciously gave one another tacit permission to cross an intimate threshold, even as strangers, perhaps because we were strangers, immersing ourselves briefly in the immensity of another's interior universe, one whose hopes, joys, questions, problems, and pain were not our own, with something good happening in the exchange. Sometimes even just being with another, without many words at all, proved to be a blessing.

One morning, I pulled up to the curb outside the train station in downtown San Diego. A young man, maybe in his twenties, smoking a cigarette privately on the sidewalk, had requested a ride. He was wearing sunglasses, a newish looking baseball cap, and a hooded sweatshirt with the hood pulled over the hat on his head. In his left hand he clenched a small blue and red duffle bag. He took his time finishing his smoke before finally sliding into the backseat, greeting me with a muffled, early-morning, "Hey."

"Hey," I replied upbeat. "How's it going?"

"Fine," he stated plainly.

It was not much banter to build on, but that was fine. I decided to wait a minute as he got situated before attempting to reengage the conversation.

"Your day off to a good start I hope?"

"Yeah, sure," he said clearing his throat.

Once on the road I could see that my passenger's destination was north of San Diego. But when I tapped the screen on my iPhone to glance at the details of the fare, I was surprised to see he was heading to a hotel mere walking distance from where I live. I couldn't believe it. Not only because of the proximity to my home but also because I could not remember ever having another passenger during the morning rush going that far north of San Diego, not once in over a thousand rides. South, sure, and east and west, too, through the various beach towns along the coast. But never north. I was genuinely curious.

"You working today?" I asked sending him a smile in the rearview mirror.

"Uh, yes. I'm working today," he said glancing up for a moment from his smartphone.

"What kind of work do you do?" I asked.

He let out a loud exhale of annoyance before answering, "I'm a porn star."

He said it so matter-of-factly it caught me off guard. I thought he might be joking. But the silence and seriousness following his admission indicated otherwise.

"Did you say porn star?" I asked. "Really?"

"Yup," he replied irritated and looking out his window.

I was flabbergasted. To date I had chauffeured a neuroscience architect, a stab victim, a former host of Dateline NBC, a UFC fighter, teachers, nurses, doctors, scientists, jurists, mothers, fathers, sons, daughters, dogs, and even just a box once with no passenger attached. But this was new. Before I could inquire any further, my passenger explained we were heading to a hotel where he would be doing a scene that morning. Then, curtly, he said, "If it's alright with you, I'm fucking tired of having these conversations and I'd rather not talk about it."

I immediately felt a swell of remorse for having irritated my guest. His path was his own. I had not wished to disturb him with my intrigue. "Silence is golden," I replied.

As we continued our drive north, my mind swirled. If he used Uber regularly, I could only imagine the questions he must field, time and again, from other drivers. Curiosity defines us as a species, as much as reason or laughter or anything else within the cacophony of our creatureliness. When we come across someone or something that deviates from the norm, an anomaly, an eccentricity, it is nearly impossible not to take an interest. That is because we, too, flirt with deviance, or what Rumi called divine mischief. We dance back and forth between the safe and the dangerous, the routine and the racy. Though it does not get much fanfare, normalcy initially is what we covet. We feel comfortable when we fit in. Nobody wants to be a pariah. It is only once we have identified and situated ourselves within a perceived norm that then we feel comfortable stretching our bounds and testing the limits with a flair of originality and a dash of difference. Though we do not want to deviate too much from the norm, lest we be branded unsuitable for society and ostracized from our networks of belonging, secretly, we long to break free from the stranglehold of standards. We seek the nourishing thrill of creativity. Instinctually, we crave otherness before the repetitive normalcy of life numbs us to the point of oblivion. In each of us there is not only Dr. Jekyll but Mr. Hyde, not only a Bruce Banner but also an Immortal Hulk, and the relation of the one to the other is not always as we imagine. Perhaps, crustaceous normality is the real monster.

In a way I admired my passenger. From a distance I marveled in awe at his audacity. Here was someone who was living thoroughly in his body, inhabiting the deep, sensual physicality of his being, unrestrained, whereas too often I had been living in my head, restrained in religion by rules, regulations, and propriety. For a moment, with my passenger in the car, it felt as though there was a balance. The seemingly sacred and the so-called profane, together, without predetermining who was who. It is interesting that the Bible in the Song of Songs celebrates sex. Even in Genesis, sex is not excluded from the biblical affirmation that everything God created is good, indeed very good as it says. Whatever it has been called throughout the centuries, making the double-backed beast, shaking the sheets, dancing the Paphian jig, love making, from a spiritual standpoint, contrary to popular opinion, actually holds a place of prominence.

"Does it ever get old though?" I wanted to ask my passenger. The thing that quietly wears away at us, not here and there, but relentlessly, day after day, is the banality of having to do so many of the very same things over and over *ad infinitum*: making the bed one more time, mowing the lawn one more time, doing our taxes one more time, so much of everything over and over again one more time until our time comes to an end. Tedium tears at us. It is only natural to wonder then, upon encountering a porn star whose profession presumably lends itself to pleasurable repetition, if there might be a way to skirt the face of the familiar. For my part I am skeptical. Does not even the pleasure of sex, when done hundreds upon thousands of times, perhaps especially when it becomes your job, ultimately succumb to the numbness of normalcy? This is called the "the Sawyer Effect" which is any practice that turns play into work, or work into play, as when Tom Sawyer tricked his friends into whitewashing his Aunt Polly's fence for him by acting as if it were a pleasure rather than a pain.[14] Money, moreover, is sometimes the crux of the problem. Whether working and living for God, as in ministry, or working and living for sex, as in pornography, once payment for services rendered is introduced, the entire enterprise can go from electrifying to jading. Once it was a playground. Now it's your job.

We arrived at the hotel and I wished my passenger well. We were not so different I thought as he stepped out of my car and into his work for the day with a sullenness all too familiar from my final days in the church. He was just steps removed from where I live, another double entendre. He thanked me for the quiet ride, and I drove away somehow graced by the encounter. A person has a distinct presence, an ethos that exudes, oozing through the pores quite apart from how much or how little is spoken. Being in the presence of others, like this other, and so many others during my time Ubering was healing. To allow ourselves to be touched by otherness enriches the soul by careening our awareness with the possibility that these shoes you happen to be in need not be as they are, and

14. Pink, *Drive*, 36–40.

might not have been as they are. Part of the joy is the anticipation of the unknown in the mystery of your own becoming.

The joy I discovered in driving my passengers to and from various and sundry places was contrary to much of what I had learned. I was not seeking happiness, yet happiness had found a way to me. I had stopped examining my life; now, life was gently washing over me, cleansing and refreshing. This is the opposite of what many of the great wisdom teachers tell us. The unexamined life is not worth living Socrates said. Seek and you will find Jesus taught. Yet seeking and examining, even the Ignatian Examen, it seems will only get you so far. There is delightful irony in that so often you only find what you are looking for after you give up pursuing it. Surrender is a hidden pathway opening onto breathtaking vistas the direct approach can never bring you. "You will never be happy if you continue to search for what happiness consists of," observed Albert Camus, "you will never live if you are looking for the meaning of life."[15] As logical as it seems to come at something like life or happiness directly, understanding them so that one might more clearly seek them, Camus reminds us that such analytics too often steer us in the wrong direction. Happiness is too elusive, too playful, to sit still while we attempt to pick it apart in order to seize upon it. Happiness is also an overinflated idea, often becoming the end-all of our desires, and thus masking the truth that happiness is not a large enough concept to contain all the human heart longs for in life: freedom, mystery, raw and radical becoming. Life, likewise, is too wildly rich to be experienced by way of dissecting its possible meanings. The direct approach of examining life and seeking happiness are found wanting. Much like our missing car keys that show up only after we forgo our frantic morning search around the house, curiously, surrendering the search for happiness and life's meaning is likewise a backward, unexpected path leading us to life indirectly. Not life apart from misery, pain, boredom, and confusion. But life with these darker shades, invited into our psyches and into hearts, where they long to dwell anyway, despite our persistent attempts at rejecting them. Happiness cannot be had apart from

15. Camus, *Intuitions*, 156.

these darker shades also coloring the canvas of our lives; midnight black, brown, and gray are there on our palettes as much as bright red, orange, and yellow beckoning for integration in the beautiful albeit messy amalgamation of the portrait that is you.

My thirteen-year-old daughter and I went for a walk around the mountain the other day. I have long delighted in my conversations with Bella. She exhibits a sparkling curiosity and hearty enthusiasm for life, in part because so much of life is continually new to her, never before tasted or seen, and also in part because of the specialness she knows in being a child, reminiscent of something Jesus once touched upon in a conversation with his disciples saying, "Unless you change and become like little children, you will never enter the kingdom of heaven."[16] Like a river winding, my morning conversation with Bella flowed from one topic to another to another. We discussed her tumbling routines for cheerleading one moment and in the same breath wondered about the possibilities of time travel. We talked best techniques for staying up all night at a sleepover and then mused over experimenting with a new pancake mix. Somehow we eventually found our way into a conversation about religion, which was somewhat unusual, not because the subject was awkward or taboo but because it had been some time since I left the church and God behind, creating an opening not only for me but for my whole family to enjoy the fresh air and free open spaces of life's hidden divinity there in our shared meals, an evening game of charades, walks around the neighborhood, and other ways in which the sacred is fully manifest yet wonderfully never named.

"You see that cross up on the hillside?" I said to Bella as we walked along.

"That's near where my friend lives," she replied.

"Yeah? Well, I don't know, maybe it's just that mischievous part of me, but I kind of wish somebody else would set up a crescent moon and star symbol, for Islam, on the opposite hillside," I said with a smile.

Bella smiled back at me. "Yeah?"

16. Matt 18:3

"Yeah," I said. "Not out of spite or anything. But because that's the reality of the world we live in. A spiritual marketplace. A plurality of faiths."

"That would probably make whoever put the cross up there mad," Bella pointed out.

"You think?"

"It might," she said. "Depending on what kind of Christians they are."

"Yes. I think you're right," I concurred. "Hopefully, if they were of the sort that took the essence of Jesus' message to heart, about love, compassion, and forgiveness, then, it wouldn't be an issue. But you might be right." The conversation paused, and we took in the sounds of the morning birds and wind combing the trees around us.

"It's projected by the year 2050 that Islam will become the world's largest religion," I said remembering an article I had seen from the Pew Research Center.

"Really?" Bella asked.

"Yes. Christianity has been the largest world religion for I don't know how many hundreds of years. But it looks like Islam will finally surpass it. And the primary reason, interestingly, is not because they are making more converts or something like that. It's because Muslim families by and large are just having more babies."

"Huh," Bella exclaimed.

"I know," I said with emphasis, smiling. "I don't know if it is in the Qur'an or if it is part of Muslims' cultural heritage or a combination of both or something else entirely but that's the primary reason why Islam is set to become the world's largest religion. Buddhism, by contrast, is the only religion that won't grow at all by 2050. Buddhists are like, 'Here we are everyone, meditating. Come and join us. Or don't. We don't care,'" I said jokingly. That made Bella laugh.

"I know this kid at school," Bella piped up, "whose mom is a Muslim and her dad is a Christian, and it sounds like they really love each other. They get along. Which I think is cool. But there's this other girl from my language arts class who's like, 'That's wrong! How can a Christian marry a Muslim?' And I'm like, 'What are you talking about? What's wrong with that?'"

"You know, me and mommy talk about this kind of thing now and then," I replied, "how one of the biggest problems in the world, we think, is narrowness."

"Narrowness?" Bella asked.

"Narrowness of perspective," I said, "but also narrowness of the heart. Closing yourself off to relationships that are different, or thinking your way is the only way, in religion or politics or with people, too often this is what leads to arguing, which leads to fighting, which leads to wars, which leads to death and destruction."

Bella chimed in, "Yeah, arguing. . . I mean, no one is going to convince me to believe something I don't believe with an argument."

"I agree. It may sound funny but it's like ice cream. When I was little, vanilla was my favorite flavor of ice cream. Beyond any other flavor. By far. I liked what I liked and no one was going to convince me that any other flavor was better. Now, for some other kid, living somewhere else, it was probably one of the other thirty-one flavors at Baskin-Robbins that was his favorite, and there would be no way I would convince him that vanilla was better than, say, Rocky Road."

"By the way, do you think we could get ice cream later?" Bella asked.

"I have some Ben and Jerry's Peanut Butter Cup in the fridge at home. You can have the rest of it if you want."

"Really?" she said.

"Really. And, just to finish our thoughts on all this religion stuff," I continued as Bella's interest was clearly waning and in need of a hyperjump to a new topic, "you know, vanilla isn't my favorite flavor anymore."

"It's not?"

"Nope. I'm not even sure if ice cream as a category is my favorite type of dessert. It's not that vanilla ice cream isn't still amazing. It is. It's just. . . people change. Human beings are dynamic, not static. You can believe or feel or think one thing, passionately, even for a very long time, and then, for a thousand different reasons seen and unseen, known and unknown, you change, sometimes even quite apart from a deliberate decision, change happens."

"Hmm. Well, religion doesn't usually interest me that much," Bella admitted cautiously. Then, after a moment, a new smile crept over her face. "So, dad, when do you think we'll go to Knott's Berry Farm?" And just like that our conversation happily turned the corner and flowed to another topic.

My daughter's candid admission that religion does not hold much interested for her struck me, because I see in her as well as in my son so much of the sublime that, ironically, religion centers on. Yet it is precisely this lack of interest, intellectually, conversationally, in religion, I believe, that allows for so much illumination in their lives. I have known religious people who thought more or less of you depending on how many times you used religious words like "God" or "Jesus" or "Bible" in a conversation but in whom I had great difficulty seeing much light at all. My children, by contrast, rather than talking God to death, instead of examining faith into oblivion, seem to delight themselves more easily and fully in life simply by living it. Later that morning, after our walk, Camus' words came to mind once again: "You will never live if you are looking for the meaning of life."

Children do not laboriously look for the meaning of life. They are not enthralled in endless conversations about a search for happiness. Children play. They sing. They cry. They complain. Children are masters of wonder and wildness, curiosity and folly. Children know much of happiness as they embrace life by living. Not analyzing. Not discussing. Not mentally dissecting. Whereas religious people can lose themselves all too easily in the minutia of splitting hairs over dogma and doctrine, who is right and who is wrong, who is saved and who is not, labeling what is good and what is bad, children live life not in their heads but in their bodies. They feel. Whether it is a joke that makes you laugh so hard you almost pee your pants, or you find yourself balling your eyes out because some kid pushed you off your bike for no apparent reason, as children life is not reified, objectified, or analyzed. Life is lived from the heart.

"You will never be happy if you continue to search for what happiness consists of. You will never live if you are looking for the meaning of life. In the same way the most fertile emotions will be lost to you if you insist on analyzing them. Listen to my madness," Camus says through a figure in his writing called the fool. Camus' "fool" is an ironic figure only striking us as a fool if we have lived our lives for too long in our heads. "But how can any of us get away from thinking?" we might ask in protest. That seems impossible, not to mention impractical. Indeed, Camus himself raises this very question to the fool who in turn makes Camus laugh with his witty reply. "Yes," getting away from our analytical addictions is impossible says the fool, "if one remains among the ordinary."[17] In fact, the fool himself has moved away from his own madness by becoming ordinary, temporarily, in order to discuss such things with Camus in this imaginary dialogue taking place in Camus' bedroom. But rather than becoming entangled in such convolutions, contortions, and contradictions, the fool dismisses the matter, forgetting the whole thing rather than trying to analyze it any further, saying, "why analyze, why rebel? Isn't living rebellion enough?"[18]

Then, the fool speaks again, revealing the truth he wants to share with us: "My happiness, you see, is in my ability to forget."[19]

The fool in his madness knows something of happiness, and perhaps more so than we do, Camus suggests, not because he is smarter than everyone else but much the opposite. "I am neither weak nor strong," says the fool, "I am nothing, for I do not know myself, having forgotten myself. I am happy and I come to bring you the good word. I come to tell you: Forget yourselves."[20]

Ralph Waldo Emerson had a similar intuition, noting, "The one thing we seek with insatiable desire is to forget ourselves, to be surprised out of our propriety, to lose our sempiternal memory, and to do something without knowing how or why; in short, to draw a new circle."[21] I began to notice within the circle of my own life how both remembering but also forgetting longed to play a role in the person I was becoming. Remembering, certain things, once forgotten about who I am, truly, wished to be recollected into the hearth of my being. On the other hand, remembering, which is a form of cognition, was not enough, and even more than that was not

17. Camus, *Intuitions*, 159.
18. Camus, *Intuitions*, 160.
19. Camus, *Intuitions*, 160.
20. Camus, *Intuitions*, 160.
21. Bloom, *Ralph Waldo Emerson*, 151.

entirely the right remedy. During my time away from the church and away from God I saw that for too long I had been lost inside my own head. I am reflective by nature and this has always been an important aspect of who I am. Perhaps I inherited or acquired some of this disposition from my father, who was a Harvard man, or my mother, who was a biofeedback therapist. The years I spent in undergraduate and graduate school only served to encourage this innate tendency I am sure, and, of course, reflection is not a bad thing at all in its own right. Still, I began to see in my newly discovered devotion to religious abstinence, whereas at one time I had found great delight in discussing things divine, now, I was called to a deeper and wider and greater fullness that meant forgetting, God, and those parts of myself tied up with God, a fullness that included but also exceeded happiness, by not discussing God, who cannot really be discussed anyway, at least not directly, that reality beyond reality, that great unreality better accessed simply by living, and by sensing the sublime suffused in us and in all things.

It is interesting that the foundations of the three great monotheistic religions actually prohibit the direct approach to the divine. God's name, YHWH, as revealed to Moses at the burning bush, for example, could not be used directly, only indirectly, by way of substitutionary terms such as Adonai. Similarly, it was taught that God could not be worshipped directly, only indirectly, with one exception that happened once a year, when the high priest alone would directly enter the Holy of Holies in the Jerusalem temple. It was also said that no one could look directly at the divine. Seeing God could only be done indirectly, catching glimpses of God's glory through the beauty of creation, with one notable exception, Moses, who was said to speak with God face to face, as one speaks with a friend. Even the aesthetic as recounted in the Hebrew Bible, in contrast to many other civilizations both past and present, denied the direct approach to God, abhorring direct representations of the holy as idolatrous, and preferring instead angelic art as indirect representation. Speaking of God. Worshipping God. Seeing God. The aesthetics of God. In all these ways there is a hinting at the sanctity of what we might call spiritual indirection. While at times spiritual direction may help us, through the guidance of a trusted confidant, and while at times we may also look back and realize how vital misdirection was to gaining a humbler, truer sense of self, at other times what benefits the soul most is direction that comes solely from within, an in-direction, one that trades the linguistic addictive tendency of too much naming and grasping for the delight of simply and tacitly beholding what is.

CHAPTER 5

The Death of Belonging

In myself, too, many things have perished which, I
imagined, would last for ever, and new structures have
arisen, giving birth to new sorrows and new joys. . .

—MARCEL PROUST, *IN SEARCH OF LOST TIME*

I REMEMBER AS A child walking home from school on a sun-
drenched afternoon, trying to imagine what my life would be like,
maybe thirty years down the road, as an adult, the woman I would
marry, the work I would do, the kind of person I would become. In
all my imaginings I was never able to conceive the current shape
of my life. Many things that once were are gone, vanished into
the ether of the past, while other things that now stand in their
place have risen anew, often surprisingly, as a result of the absence
of what used to be, the disappearance of one giving birth to the
emergence of another. For the longest time, I thought what I was
looking for was belonging, a place, or a way, to belong. But I was
wrong. There is the death of belonging, the sober realization that
being here, there, or anywhere in this life, fully and completely, is
not inherent to our nature. We are forever transcending. We long
for something we cannot realize. Inasmuch as beauty is despair, an
awakening in us by the glory of something beheld for a moment

before being pulled back to the simple mediocrity of so much daily living, belonging likewise teases us with the hope of a rooted stability in some imagined milieu always just beyond our reach. I thought I had discovered belonging in the drug induced days of my purple haze as a late teen, and then shortly thereafter for some time in religion, Jesus, and God. To finally see with a modicum of clarity I no longer needed to belong because I could not belong was, strangely, a way of belonging by not belonging to a truth that set me free. I felt clear and at the same time emotionally undone at an illusion I had entertained for too long.

Hate, resentment, and anger surfaced within me as dark forms of the passion I once knew for my work in the church. Even the joy of my rideshare driving began to wear thin after nine months, ready to give way to something new. The trouble was I did not know what that something new was which made it tempting to grasp at just about anything that might rescue me from waiting in the dark.

The first temptation arrived in the form of an innocuous email. A church in Colorado had acquired my name, and the chair of their search committee was personally inviting me to throw my hat in the ring for the Senior Minister position at their five-hundred-member congregation, with a minimum starting salary of one hundred thousand dollars per year. After all I had discerned about my need to leave the church, you might think I would have immediately deleted the email, and anything less than that would be symptomatic of lunacy. But when you have been without much of a salary from month to month as a rideshare driver, and your almost forgotten pastoral, professional alter ego hears about such an enticing opportunity, it is hard not to at least dig a little deeper, even if you are digging your own grave.

When I told Erin later that evening as we were getting ready for bed that I had received the email and was reading the church bio and job description, she looked at me with a combination of compassion, rage, and absolute disbelief. She did not say a single word. She did not have to. Her face said it all. After mulling it over for a day, and with some good counsel from my wife, I came to my senses and tossed the temptation aside.

A second temptation arrived a month later also by email. It proved to be twice as tempting. It was another church position and this time right around the corner from where I live. Crucially, it was an interim position of only six months, which meant no long-term commitment, just doing good for others while at the same time being able to help pay the cost of cheerleading for my daughter, chess club for my son, and our monthly rent, among other expenses. But what does someone who no longer speaks about God say during a sermon? And how does one invite others to belong to Christ and Christian community who himself no longer belongs? I am ashamed only partially to admit that I seriously considered the opportunity for four days before finally turning it down and letting it go, remembering in the process a humorous proverb from the Hebrew Bible, "Like a dog that returns to its vomit is a fool who reverts to his folly."[1]

Neither of these temptations prepared me, however, for a third temptation that came by way of a phone call. The call was from an unknown number, so I let it go to voicemail. When I listened to the message a minute later, I learned I had received an invitation to meet with the dean of the Philosophy and Religious Studies Department at a local college for a teaching position. Prior to my departure from the church, I sent off resumes to universities in the area thinking it might be a way forward. Years earlier I had taught religion and philosophy at Sacred Heart University in Connecticut before entering into full-time ministry. In retrospect, my three years teaching in academia were three of the happiest years of my life. I had been passionate about engaging students' hearts, minds, and curiosities over the great questions of life. Who are we? Where did everything come from? What is the meaning of it all? Does God exist and, if so, why is there so much suffering? The thought of returning to something I once loved now post-church seemed to make sense.

But the voicemail filled me with anticipation and fear as much as with joy. While on the one hand this seemed like an invitation worth considering, on the other hand I had been cloistered away

---

1. Prov 26:11

from most things religious in a way that felt wonderful since leaving the church, and I wondered if I still had it in me to get back in the saddle, stand at the front of a classroom full of students, and teach again.

Before returning the phone call to either accept or decline the invitation, I decided to take time to be with my fear. Fear can be a friend revealing our deepest concerns. If you are afraid of meeting a deadline at work and you sit with the fear, you may come to see that what you are really concerned about is not only the deadline but letting down your co-workers whom you care about. There is care in your fear. If you are anxious about speaking at a corporate luncheon and you befriend the fear, you may find courage in the midst of your vulnerability and decide the value of what you have to say complements your anxieties about presentation. There is authenticity in your fear.

As I sat with the enticing but terrifying thought of teaching again I realized I could do it if I wanted to do it because indeed I had done it. If anything, I was even more prepared from the lessons I had learned from my past failures and successes in the classroom. The fear, I discerned, was mostly heightened timidity after having been out of academia for some time. Seeing that I realized fear alone would be a poor reason to turn down the opportunity.

I called the dean's office and told the friendly administrative assistant who answered the phone I would love to learn more. The following Monday morning at nine o'clock I found myself sitting down with the dean, discussing the ins and outs of the position, talking pedagogy, answering "what if" scenarios, and learning, to my surprise, that though this was a part-time faculty position there was the possibility of it developing into a full-time, tenure track position. "If you're interested in that sort of thing," the dean added, looking for my response. In the blink of an eye, I found myself contemplating the joy of having a "regular" job again, one that would make use of my degrees and skill set and pay substantially better than what I was making as a rideshare driver. I thought about how much I enjoyed teaching in the past and wondered if it could be the same again. I also knew the chance at a full-time faculty position in any college or university is extremely difficult to come by these days. In that moment my ambitious, firstborn self was tickled pink at the possibility and, without time to spare, I nonchalantly told the dean, "Yes, I think I would be interested in that sort of thing."

After the meeting, I was off to the races. I received a phone call later that night informing me I had secured the position. I had two short weeks to prepare a syllabus and lesson plans for a class on World Religions. Over the next several days I began pulling out old resources I had saved and, most importantly, resurrecting, if possible, an old academic self that had been buried for years. Part of me knew I might be accepting a position like this far too soon, thereby eliminating precious time for healing, rest, and reflection I was enjoying since my departure from ministry. But I also knew that by trying on this temptation I would have the opportunity to explore a once trodden path I might happily walk again. In academia, I would be talking *about* religion without many of the more subjective assumptions that go along with doing religious work in the church. I also felt really good about doing something I was qualified for, meaning that time, money, and effort spent earning my undergraduate and graduate degrees would not be wasted. My mental calculations seemed to add up, and the job felt like a close enough parallel to what I had been doing in ministry without being too close. It turns out I was completely wrong.

Exactly one week after accepting the job I realized I made a horrible mistake. The realization was especially painful because it did not come in the form of a gradual revelation. The revelation was cascading, as if I was standing at the bottom of a waterfall being hit with the hundred ton full elemental force of the knowledge that I needed to stop, and stop now, before the semester began, and before I was drowning in something that was not me, not anymore.

The cascading began at dinner. I had spent the last several days tirelessly crafting new lesson plans, selecting reading materials for the course, researching, thinking, and envisioning what it was going to be like to actually do this. My orientation process with the college's human resources department, and a forty-one-page admissions packet, were complete, with texts already being ordered for students through the bookstore for what was shaping up to be a class of fifty. Then, at dinner, after finishing my lesson planning for the day, my lovely wife asked me a most innocent question. Glancing at me with her soft eyes Erin said, "Did you enjoy your work today?"

The question, like cannon fire, echoed in my head, and gave rise to panic in my heart. Hmm. Did I enjoy my work today? Over the past week there had been moments I enjoyed, sure. As I thought about it, however, I realized what I enjoyed the most was only the possibility of doing something other than rideshare driving, work that had the facade of greater nobility. Seeing this I was deeply embarrassed, and could not give Erin a direct answer to her question. I felt an intense and desperate need to turn away: from my family at the dinner table, my piles of work in the living room, and to go for a walk, alone, near Lake Hodges along the back roads of our neighborhood.

I burned as I walked, the night air cooling, barely able to think a single coherent thought, a good thing, actually, because being in my head was not what I needed most in that moment. My emotions needed to speak. Sometimes, all the truth needs is a walk around the lake.[2] Though it was hard to admit, I saw that being a professor, appearances aside, was not me anymore, much like being a pastor was not me anymore, and thus there was not going to be any real joy down this path. Joy is a reality of resonance. If there is dissonance between you and a pursuit, or you and a person, and you persist, ultimately, you frustrate your own happiness. But, by listening to yourself, your fears, your hopes, what you love and what you hate, gradually, you begin discerning not only if a path is for you, you will know if a path is you.

As I walked along with the moon overhead, I thought about the boards and committees I would need to serve on at the college. It was made clear during my meeting with the dean that such administrative duties were part of the job, which, honestly, sounded less than thrilling. I also thought about what becoming a full-time faculty member would entail long-term, namely, teaching a substantial number of classes online, I was told, not working in a traditional classroom with students, though that was my real joy.

2. Stevens, *The Collected Poems*, 408.

Short-term as well, when I looked closely at what I would be teaching, lesson by lesson, I had to confess, I simply was not interested in studying religion anymore.

As I walked, I recalled some dark dreams I had over the past week since accepting the position, dreams I had brushed under the rug and purposefully not allowed to speak their truth. They were downright gruesome. One dream involved me strapped down to a wooden-style torture table, apparently by my doppelganger, with me standing above myself, mutilating myself, my evil twin managing to do his worst using mangled hands that for some reason had been turned into ground beef using an electric beater. The dream was so disturbing I refused to ruminate on it. At least that was my initial rationale. When I finally came around to the dream on my walk, however, what I saw was all too obvious: the work I had been furiously engaged in to prepare for my class was a covert act of self-violence.

Later, after I finished walking, and finally fell asleep just before dawn, exhausted by the cascading of the evening, I had a different kind of dream. A mother was holding hands with her daughter, a cute little girl no older than five, with curly dark hair. They were walking along a trail in the mountains, and then, the mother was saying goodbye to her little girl. She was giving her away. The scene should have been sad. But it was not. Somehow, the little girl knew, as her mother did, it was time to go. Upon waking, though strange, I knew the little girl and the mother were versions of me. The psychologist Carl Jung taught that there are feminine and masculine principles in everyone, regardless of sex. These principles of *anima* (female) and *animus* (male) often show up in your dreams. The female dimension of *anima* is a creative source, enabling you in your nightlife to conceive new possibilities, personas, and pathways. In my dream, I realized I was letting go of belonging, to a version of myself, one that had been teacherly for a time, a death that at the same time was fallow ground for the possibility of new birth.

The following day I contacted the dean and rescinded my acceptance of the position. I also learned the previous night had been a full moon. In a curious way it felt almost as if the moon had somehow pulled me, moved and caressed me, into seeing a truth

I needed to see. It is interesting that the word "lunacy" is derived from the Latin word *luna*, meaning moon, though you certainly do not have to be a madman to know there are measurable lunar effects on both people and the planet. The actual geophysical environment of the earth morphs because of the moon, impressively, with our North American continent rising as much as half a foot in the moon's presence. The gravitational pull of the moon shifts the tides of the oceans of course, too, but also our biological tides. This is not very surprising given the majority of the human body, like the surface of the earth, is composed of water. Ancient exaggerations of shifts in the human experience during full moons include lycanthropy, better known as werewolfism, and though such claims are fantastic, it is easy to see how such an idea could take root when today there are documented cases of increased agitation and even aggression relative to the lunar cycle. In Dade County, Florida, for example, from 1956 to 1970, homicide rates spiked well above normal during new moons and full moons, with the same correlation observed in Cuyahoga County, Ohio from 1958 to 1970.[3] I did not need graphs and charts, however, while working the nightshift at a Mobil gas station during my college years to see with my own two eyes how business got a little weird whenever the moon was big and bright overhead.

Whatever correlation there might have been between the moon and my emotive state that night I am grateful for what I learned. By resisting the temptation to enter academia again, as well as two previous temptations to re-enter the ministry, and as my rideshare driving gradually became more painful than joyful and trickled off, in the waiting, I began to catch glimpses of a raw and dark emotionality beneath the surface of my self, one I might not have noticed, and one I had not the faintest inkling of its existence or extent. I realized I was full of hate.

It was horribly painful, accepting the presence of this hate. There was so much of it. Once noticed, however, I could not take my eyes off it. It was vast, beyond what I ever could have imagined, like a red seething lake of lava that had been gathering, waiting for

---

3. Lieber, *The Lunar Effect*, 15–30, 67–89.

some time to find a fissure and burst forth. What seemed like a life-time ago I had fallen in love not only with Jesus but with love itself, Jesus' greatest command to his disciples, and I had become so utter-ly committed to the calling to love others, no matter what, that the notion of its dark counterpart lurking deep within was more than a little unsettling. The volcanism seared, physically making me hot at times, longing for nothing more than exposure, acknowledgement, too fiery to be touched, tooled, or analyzed. When we feel angry or anxious, depressed or full of fear, the temptation is to want to "do" something with these dark emotions. Yet letting them be and have their own way with us is sometimes how we learn the most.

In May of 1980, Mount St. Helens erupted in Washington state killing 57 people along with millions of livestock and wild-life. "Suddenly I could see nothing," comments one eyewitness, "I'd been knocked down and my hard hat blown off. It got hot right away, then scorching hot and impossible to breathe. The air had no oxygen, like being trapped underwater. . . I was being cremated, the pain unbearable."[4] It is amazing how something as thoroughly destructive as a volcano, its molten hot magma spewing forth from secret canals deep in the earth, can also then lay the groundwork for life. Less than a year after the eruption, scientists were already discovering new life growing from the gray ash. This phoenix phe-nomenon is due in part to the fact that volcanic ash helps to make incredibly fertile soil, containing high concentrations of minerals, lower pH levels, and high moisture retention rates, all things many plants prefer. Fire is both a destroyer and bearer of life.

Personally, the more I allowed myself to behold the ire of my hate, the more I knew myself to be standing in the presence of something real, dangerous, and, at the same time, creative. If there is a time for love, there is a time for hate, and though the hate burned, simply beholding its elemental power and presence was akin to an act of truth-telling, a form of release through acceptance. It is tempting to label something like hate as evil, and it is easy to point to hate crimes in the headlines as evidence of hate's toxicity. But just as there are many shades of love, such as *eros* (passionate

4. Waitt, *In the Path of Destruction*, 164.

love) and *agape* (unconditional love) and *philia* (friendship love) so, too, hate has many faces, functions, and forms. Hate like love is nuanced, multifarious. In the Bible, in Ecclesiastes, where we find the famous teaching that there is a time and a season for all things, it is interesting that the Hebrew primitive root for the word "hate" (*sane*) means to detest, to turn against, to turn away. By contrast the Hebrew primitive root for the word "love" (*aheb*) means beloved, to befriend, to turn towards. Hate, in other words, etymologically and biblically, at a most elementary level, is a natural dynamic, as normal as the ebb and flow of the tides, as necessary as the exhaling is to the inhaling of breathing. As essential as it is at times for you to turn towards something, or someone, at other times it can be just as vital for you to turn away. Leaving God was a necessary turning—away—functioning as an emotionally intuitive self-defense mechanism: I had reached a turning point, where for so long I had been turning towards so many people in ministry and in my life, turning towards so many needs, so often and so much, that now a season and a time had arrived to gracefully turn away.

My turning away was less an act of wisdom, though, and more out of impotence. The fiery reservoir of my hate was so emotionally immense and intense that there was nothing else for me to do but let it be, something we often find incredibly difficult to do with vital sources of energy in our interior life, letting things be. We are more apt to toy and tinker, manipulate and mold that which has even an aura of power. Yet learning to let be the bright and dark pedagogies of our interiority opens us to a fuller infusion of forces that resist our naïve attempts to place reigns on the wild within. Letting things be is at once impossibly difficult and incredibly simple. If you are angry, be angry. If you are happy, even over the smallest unexpected joy in your day, be happy. By beginning with what is, rather than a judgment on your emotive state, or a presumed moral imperative about what to do with it, you anchor your head, heart, and habits in the truth of your own experience, whatever that experience might be. This is good grounding for the soul. The soul craves truth, whatever the truth might be and regardless of how it looks or sounds to others, bright or dark, cool or searing. Letting be the beauty, balance, and fluidity of nature's essential dynamics within you is the seedbed of authentic, integrated living. Fierce with reality, you begin living free, as you are free from the shackles of presumption and posturing. There is blessedness in being brave enough to live your own life according to the simple truth of what is within you.

As I gave myself over to the apprenticeship of my hate, I observed the fire bringing warmth and illumination to my understanding, not only wrath and rage. Late one night, when I could not sleep, I sat with the hate, in the dark, on the floor in my living room for some time. Though most of the time it was inscrutable with no focal point, a broad-ranging disappointment with life, that so much changes, and quite often without our consult or consent, on this night as it flared, I felt filled with hate at being a failure—as a father. My children and I used to pray together. Now we do not. We used to meditate in the morning. Now we do not. We used to read the Bible. Now we do not. As I sat with the incinerating shame, the hate burning, and purifying, eventually, I saw something surprising: I am not failing my beloved Bella and Joshua, or anyone else for that matter, not if I am showing them me. Beyond spiritual exercises of prayer and mindfulness and reading sacred texts, beyond belief and disbelief and whatever lies in between, there is nothing, absolutely nothing that can replace the gift of your authentic becoming. To share the truth of your own being and becoming with another is as real as it gets, and there is no better bond or basis for our relationships than the real.

Postscript

The greatest honor we can pay to God is
to leave God alone and so be free of God.
Only then can we be true beyond all our
knowing and desiring, and only then
can we find ourselves and
let God be God.

—MEISTER ECKHART, *BOOK OF THE HEART*

WE LIKE HAPPY ENDINGS. When my kids and I saw the blockbuster *Avengers: Infinity War* in theaters opening night, we were absolutely devastated, along with everyone else at the screening, when the evil Thanos won, and half of all Marvel's superheroes and half of all life in the universe died. Attending San Diego Comic-Con later that summer, we got a laugh out of the tongue-in-cheek counseling station Marvel set up in a parking lot for fans having a hard time with the movie's not-so-happy ending. At least everyone knew the film's sequel *Avengers: Endgame* would come to theatres the following summer. There was hope.

The history of faith in a similar way in the Judeo-Christian tradition is characterized by an array of anticlimactic, only tentatively hopeful endings. In the final chapter of the most ancient gospel, the Gospel of Mark, ending in verse 8, which scholars agree is the original ending, we find some of the disciples visiting Jesus' tomb, discovering it empty, and leaving, afraid, saying nothing to anyone.

To be sure there is a messenger in the tomb, providing some hope, stating Jesus has risen. Yet we are left with only his words, and a missing messiah.[1] Jonah, too, offers us a less than satisfying ending to his whale of a tale in the Hebrew Bible. After finally agreeing to do what God calls him to do, traveling to the city of Nineveh and warning the people to change their ways, instead of feeling fulfilled, Jonah is angry, "angry enough to die," he says.[2] The story then ends with a question mark, not exactly the Hollywood happy ending we are accustomed to.

Moses, too, is a paragon of incompleteness. After his extended battle with the Pharaoh, and then the toil of leading his people through the wilderness of Sinai, Moses dies, no less than at the very edge of the Promised Land, not able to enjoy it himself, only able to see it for a moment, at a distance.[3] Similarly, the New Testament Letter to the Hebrews recounts person after person—Rahab, Gideon, Barak, Samson, Jephthah, David, Samuel, the prophets, and more—all of whom were commended for their faith yet not one received what was promised.[4]

This is a curious message that we find in the Bible, one I find comforting, as it meshes with my own experience of faith. It is a message rooted in realism, one that moves beyond equating faithfulness with happiness. The journey of faith with God and beyond is marked as much by tentativeness as assurance, frustration as fulfillment, a comma as much as a period. Joy is not excluded from the journey, and neither are hate, melancholy, love, hope, or the menagerie of other elements that make us human. There is an invitation for all.

Late one sleepless night, I stumbled upon a YouTube video about another individual, like myself, taking his own leap of faith. The man had traded a very nice eighty thousand dollar a year job to work instead at a grocery store. This was no small decision on his part. After graduating from college, he had acquired a respectable

1. Mark 16:1–8
2. Jonah 4:9
3. Deut 34:1–5
4. Heb 11:39

government job, and before long was doing quite well for himself personally and financially. He bought a large four-bedroom house in the suburbs, and soon acquired a taste for elegant furnishings, regularly redecorating his place with new purchases, eventually selling his home to upgrade in his mind to an even better one. Each year at the company he received a raise for his hard work, an incentive large enough to keep him engaged and moving forward, and, after eleven years, he had more than a few luxuries including a pair of golden handcuffs. Benefits, a fat pension, and a big salary meant he never really had to think about money. He had a lot of freedom: to shop, purchase, and impress his houseguests with fancy microfiber couches and the like. He also possessed the deepening knowledge that he wasn't really happy. He would come home from work, drained of his essence, feeling more than only physically depleted, dreading going back the next day. He did not understand how he could feel so debilitated because, on the surface, his work did not look all that difficult. Yet sitting in an office, in front of a computer screen for eight hours a day, was somehow exhausting. Finally, having enough of it, and after flipping out one day, he says, he took a leap of faith. He quit. Despite family and friends telling him he was crazy to be giving up so much, he let it all go. It was the forsaking not only of a job but the bittersweet loss of an identity. Then, after enjoying a ten-day silent retreat, to gain clarity about what he really wanted out of his life, he began a new chapter. Now he enjoys working part-time in a grocery store just down the street from his minimalist one-bedroom apartment. He also enjoys the fresh air and exercise of biking to and from work, as a car is no longer a necessity for him. He of course needs to watch his monthly budget more closely, too, and he continues to struggle with personal challenges like anyone. Life is not perfect. Now, however, he is happier, as he has more time for what really matters to him: time with friends, time for his interests and hobbies, and time for attending to his own personal growth. The change, though difficult, was one of the best decisions of his life.

As it came to a close the video made me smile sitting there in the dark. Though it had been a trying day, I found solace in being reminded once more that my journey is not a solitary one.

Since leaving God behind and beginning again life is different in many ways. My family now lives in a lovely little apartment half the size of our previous home. Retirement savings are on hold. Our monthly budget is modest, larger than some and humbler than others. I am currently contemplating work in hospice or hospital chaplaincy. The future is open, uncertain as ever, and, I am happier. Most days. Other days there is chaos constellating inside me. I am both more settled and unsettled in my own being, with a greater appreciation for the beauty, complexity, and wildness of my own nature and indeed life itself. Saint John of the Cross once said the soul makes the most progress, not when everything is simple and clear, but when you are traveling in darkness, unknowing.[5] We do not have to be found or figured out to enjoy life's fullness. Being in rhythm with the mystery of your own becoming is gift enough.

5. John of the Cross, *Dark Night of the Soul*, 84.

Bibliography

Alighieri, Dante. *Inferno*. Translated by Allen Mandelbaum. New York: Bantam, 1980.

Camus, Albert. *Youthful Writings*. Translated by Ellen Conroy Kennedy. New York: Alfred A. Knopf, 1976.

Christensen, Michael J. and Rebecca Laird. *The Heart of Henri Nouwen: His Words of Blessing*. New York: Crossroad, 2017.

Emerson, Ralph Waldo. *Nature, Addresses, and Lectures*. Cambridge: Riverside, 1876.

———. *Ralph Waldo Emerson*, edited by Harold Bloom. New York: Chelsea House, 2007.

Ewing, Al. *Immortal Hulk Vol. 1: Or Is He Both?* New York: Marvel, 2018.

Hildegard of Bingen. "Speaking to the Soul." https://www.episcopalcafe.com/speaking-to-the-soul-hildegard-of-bingen-woman-of-strength-and-wisdom/.

Jacobson, Howard. *The Dog's Last Walk: (and Other Pieces)*. London: Bloomsbury, 2017.

Jenkins, Paul. *Inhumans*. New York: Marvel, 2013.

Lieber, Arnold L. *The Lunar Effect: Biological Tides and Human Emotions*. New York: Doubleday, 1978.

Linn, Dennis, Sheila Linn, and Matthew Linn. *Sleeping with Bread: Holding What Gives You Life*. Mahwah: Paulist, 1995.

McWhorter, John. *The Story of Human Language: Part I*. Chantilly: The Teaching Company, 2004.

Mlodinow, Leonard. *The Drunkard's Walk: How Randomness Rules Our Lives*. New York: Pantheon, 2008.

Moore, Thomas. *Care of the Soul: A Guide for Cultivating Depth and Sacredness in Everyday Life*. New York: HarperCollins, 1992.

Murakami, Haruki. *1Q84*. Translated by Jay Rubin and Philip Gabriel. New York: Alfred A. Knopf, 2011.

Novak, Michael. *The Experience of Nothingness: Revised and Expanded Edition*. New Brunswick: Transaction, 1998.

O'Donohue, John. *Eternal Echoes: Celtic Reflections on Our Yearning to Belong.* New York: Harper Perennial, 2000.

Palmer, Parker. *Let Your Life Speak: Listening for the Voice of Vocation.* San Francisco: Jossey-Bass, 2000.

Pink, Daniel H. *Drive: The Surprising Truth About What Motivates Us.* New York: Riverhead, 2009.

Plato, *Phaedrus.* Translated by Benjamin Jowett. Chicago: R.R. Donnelley & Sons, 1983.

Porter, Roy. *Madness: A Brief History.* Oxford: Oxford University Press, 2002.

Proust, Marcel. *In Search of Lost Time.* Translated by C.K. Scott Moncrieff and Sydney Schiff. 7 vols. New York: Centaur, 2016.

Rogers, Ben. *Pascal.* New York: Routledge, 1999.

Saint John of the Cross. *Dark Night of the Soul.* Translated by E. Allison Peers. Mineola: Dover, 2008.

Solnit, Rebecca. *Wanderlust: A History of Walking.* New York: Viking Penguin, 2000.

Stevens, Anthony. *Ariadne's Clue: A Guide to the Symbols of Humankind.* Princeton: Princeton University Press, 1999.

Stevens, Wallace. *The Collected Poems: The Corrected Edition.* New York: Vintage, 2015.

Stone, Douglas and Shelia Heen. *Thanks for the Feedback: The Science and Art of Receiving Feedback Well (Even When It Is Off Base, Unfair, Poorly Delivered, and, Frankly, You're Not in the Mood).* New York: Penguin, 2014.

Sweeney, Jon M. and Mark S. Burrows. *Meister Eckhart's Book of the Heart: Meditations for the Restless Soul.* Charlottesville: Hampton Roads, 2017.

Taylor, Barbara Brown. *Learning to Walk in the Dark.* San Francisco: HarperOne, 2015.

Thoreau, Henry David. *Essays: A Fully Annotated Edition,* edited by Jeffrey S. Cramer. New Haven: Yale University Press, 2013.

Waitt, Richard. *In the Path of Destruction: Eyewitness Chronicles of Mount St. Helens.* Pullman: Washington State University Press, 2015.

Walsch, Neale Donald. Facebook post, July 22, 2014. https://www.facebook. com/NealeDonaldWalsch/photos/a.400017592343181782.40638047343/ 10152199231662344/?type=3&theater.

Whyte, David. "What to Remember When Waking: The Disciplines of an Everyday Life." Sounds True (May 2010). No pages. Audiobook.

Wilson, Paul Scott. *Setting Words on Fire: Putting God at the Center of the Sermon.* Nashville: Abingdon, 2008.

Wittgenstein, Ludwig. *Culture and Value.* Translated by Peter Winch. Chicago: University of Chicago Press, 1980.

———. *Philosophical Investigations.* 3rd ed. Translated by G.E.M. Anscombe. London: Pearson, 1973.